WHO SWITCHED OFF
MY
BRAIN?

controlling **toxic** thoughts and emotions

dr. caroline leaf

For further information please contact
Dr. Caroline Leaf by visiting www.drleaf.net
or write to the office of Dr. Leaf.

2140 E Southlake Blvd.
Suite L #809
Southlake, TX 76092

Distributed by Thomas Nelson Publishers,
printed in the United States of America.

ISBN: 978-0-9819567-2-5

Disclaimer: The information and solutions offered in this book are intended
to serve as guidelines for managing toxic thoughts, emotions and bodies.
Please discuss specific symptoms and medical conditions with your doctor.

Inprov, Ltd. with licensing permission from Switch On Your Brain USA LP

INPROV

DEDICATION

To Jesus Christ:
My Lord and Savior, my source
of inspiration and strength

To my husband, Mac:
My ever-present loving support, you are
an outstanding example of controlling
toxic thoughts and emotions

To my children:
Jessica, Dominique, Jeffrey-John and Alexandria,
you are my absolute joy and a
complete guide to detoxing

ENDORSEMENTS

"Thank God for Dr. Leaf who is able to give such clarity to the complex subject of our brain and how we think, truly helping us understand how our thoughts impact our outlook on life and affect our physical body as well. *Who Switched Off My Brain?* is fascinating reading with insight into how changing your thinking will change your emotions, your health and, ultimately, your life!" - James Robison

"I have made extensive use of Dr. Leaf's insightful book, *Who Switched Off My Brain?: Toxic Thoughts, Emotions and Bodies,* in achieving better outcomes in my patients."
- Dr. Sterna Franzsen, MD

"Dr Caroline Leaf's gift is explaining the mind-body connection in understandable terms. I enjoyed this book as a medical doctor, neuroscientist and as a person seeking optimal health in spirit, soul and body. My advice to anyone reading this book is to digest it, meditate on it and apply it."
- Dr. Peter Amua-Quarshie, MD

"2 Corinthians 10:5 tells us to take every thought captive, and I have always stepped out in faith and believed that. I am so grateful to Dr. Caroline Leaf, because I now understand how science lines up with the effectiveness of daily principles God has laid out for us in His Word. *Who Switched Off My Brain?* has practical applications for detoxing our thought life and important keys for each of us to break free from our hurts, habits and hang-ups." - Marilyn Hickey

TABLE OF CONTENTS

LETTER FROM THE AUTHOR

This is such an exciting time!

As scientists, we now understand so much more about how our thoughts affect our emotions and bodies. Because we can see clearly how brain science lines up with Scripture, we can also start breaking the chains of toxic thinking in a dynamic way, proving that your mind can be renewed, toxic thoughts and emotions can be swept away, and your brain really can be "switched on."

When the first edition of *Who Switched Off My Brain?* was published in South Africa, I was completely unprepared for the overwhelming response. As I started to receive letters and emails from people who found freedom from their past and were stepping confidently into wholeness in their thinking, learning, and emotions, I began to realize that people from every age group and every part of the world were seeking something similar – a way to break unhealthy thought patterns. The desire for freedom from toxic thinking is universal.

That's why I'm so passionate about this expanded edition of *Who Switched Off My Brain?*. You really can overcome toxic thinking and its effects. You really can renew and refresh your mind. Not only does Scripture uphold this principle, but science proves when we work with how our brains are wired, lasting, life-giving change really is possible.

As we go on this journey of understanding the science of thought by breaking toxic thinking in twelve areas of our lives, it is my hope that you find freedom.

It is also important to recognize the necessity of consulting a medical professional for comprehensive care, especially if you are experiencing any serious medical issues. In no way do I want this book to substitute for the care of a medical professional.

I believe everyone can find freedom in their thought lives, and because of this, I have tried to take complex science and bring it to life in an easy-to-understand way. Brain research and the science of thought and communication are very broad fields, and this book provides an overview, a window into the incredible world of the mind, instead of a full technical and neurobiological survey. For this reason, I have compiled a list at the end of this book with some additional resources that I have used for my own research over the years, should you wish to continue studying this on your own.

Love,
Dr. Caroline Leaf

1 PART ONE
SWITCH ON YOUR BRAIN!

We use our powerful God-tools for smashing
warped philosophies, tearing down barriers
erected against the truth of God, fitting every
loose thought and emotion and impulse
into the structure of life shaped by Christ.
2 Corinthians 10:5 (The Message)

1
CHAPTER
INTRODUCTION

Do you ever feel like your brain has just been "switched off"? Have you ever felt discouraged, unfocused or overwhelmed? Are there unhealthy patterns in your life or your family that you just can't seem to break?

Thankfully, we are living in a time of revolution. We now have a better understanding than ever before of how our thoughts affect our emotions and bodies. We can see clearly how brain science lines up with Scripture – that your mind can be renewed, that toxic thoughts and emotions can be swept away and that your brain really can be "switched on."

Toxic thoughts are like poison, but the good news is, you can break the cycle of toxic thinking. You can reverse the affects of toxic thoughts. And once that cycle of toxic thinking has been broken, your thoughts can actually start to improve every area of your life – your relationships, your health and even your success.[1]

A thought may seem harmless, but if it becomes toxic, even just a thought can become physically, emotionally or spiritually dangerous.

Thoughts are measurable and occupy mental "real estate." Thoughts are active; they grow and change. Thoughts influence every decision, word, action and physical reaction we make.[2]

AN ACTIVE THOUGHT

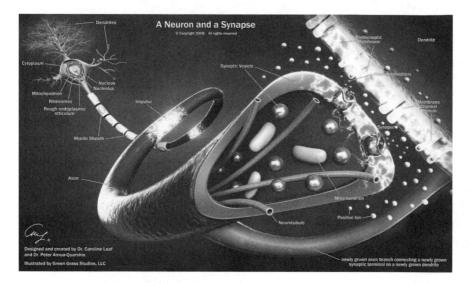

Every time you have a thought, it is actively changing your brain and your body – for better or for worse.

There are twelve areas of toxic thoughts – a disruptive crew I call the "Dirty Dozen" – which can be as harmful as poison in our minds and our bodies. Toxic thoughts don't just creep into our minds as a result of abuse or an especially horrific trauma. Toxic thoughts affect people in all stages of life, in every part of the world, every day. Even something as small as a minor irritation can become toxic, and these thoughts need to be swept away.

 Let me introduce you to The Dirty Dozen, areas of our lives targeted by toxic thinking:

- Toxic Thoughts
- Toxic Emotions
- Toxic Words
- Toxic Choices
- Toxic Dreams

- Toxic Seeds
- Toxic Faith
- Toxic Love
- Toxic Touch
- Toxic Seriousness
- Toxic Health
- Toxic Schedules

The result of toxic thinking translates into stress in your body, and this type of stress is far more than just a fleeting emotion. Stress is a global term for the extreme strain on your body's systems as a result of toxic thinking. It harms the body and the mind in a multitude of ways from patchy memory to severe mental health, immune system problems, heart problems and digestive problems.[3]

No system of the body is spared when stress is running rampant. A massive body of research collectively shows that up to 80% of physical, emotional and mental health issues today could be a direct result of our thought lives.[4] But there is hope. You can break the cycle of toxic thinking and start to build healthy patterns that bring peace to a stormy thought life.[5]

We don't have to allow the Dirty Dozen and their partners in crime (mental and physical diseases) to invade the privacy of our brains and bodies any more than we would allow an intruder to invade the privacy of our homes. We are equipped to detox and develop the potential of our magnificent brains.

People often ask me, "Why haven't I heard about toxic thinking before?"

The answer is simple; we are living in a revolutionary time for the science of thought. When I first started to research the brain more than twenty years ago, the scientific community did not embrace the direct link between the science of thought and its effects on the body. If doctors couldn't find a cause for an illness, many times the default answer was, "It's all in your head." This phrase came with a social stigma because when it came to the psychiatric perspective, most mental illnesses were not seen as having a biological base.[6]

The common wisdom of the time was that the brain is like a machine, and if a part broke, it couldn't be repaired. It was believed that the brain was hardwired from birth with a fixed destiny to wear out with age. Adding this belief to the assumption that we were bound to a fate predetermined by our genes made the horizon of hope seem bleak.

As you can imagine, these assumptions led to many common conclusions about the best ways to overcome the most difficult experiences, conclusions which were not based on how the brain functions. But we are no longer bound by those misperceptions. You are not a victim of biology.[7] God has given us a design of hope: we can switch on our brains, renew our minds, change and heal.

Because I was taught at an early age that change for the better was always a possibility, when I joined the scientific community, I found the negative outlook difficult to understand. I thought there must be something more that we could do to reach children with learning disabilities, patients with head injuries, and people desperate for peace in their minds.

Then, as I explored the archives of brain research, I started finding studies from respected scientists suggesting the brain really can change, grow and get better – that this limited mind-body distinction was not an accurate understanding of the mighty brain. I reached the same conclusions as I did my own research: science really does prove thoughts can be measured, they affect every area of our life, and best of all, the brain really can change.[8]

Now a revolution is sweeping through the field of brain science like never before.[9] The greatest part for me as a scientist is that it all lines up with God's precepts. I am so excited that we get to be a part of one of the most thrilling science adventures of mankind – understanding the "true you." I want to show you through godly scientific eyes that will encourage, rather than shatter, your hopes and help you realize you have an amazing brain filled with real physical thoughts that you can control.

2
CHAPTER
WHAT IS A TOXIC THOUGHT?

What are "toxic thoughts," and how are they different from
healthy thoughts? Toxic thoughts are thoughts that trigger
negative and anxious emotions, which produce biochemicals
that cause the body stress. They are stored in your mind,
as well as in the cells in your body.

There are twelve areas of toxic thinking – also called the
Dirty Dozen. This motley crew is always up to no good
and can cause serious damage, which is why they need to
be swept away. The "Brain Sweep" I've developed will do
just that! It is a series of sequential questions that will take
your brain through a detoxing process.

In Part Four of this book, we will meet each of the Dirty
Dozen individually, and the Brain Sweep questions will help
you sweep away that area of toxic thinking. It really is quite
simple, because the process is based on how your brain
actually works!

The surprising truth is that every single thought – whether
it is positive or negative – goes through the same cycle when
it forms. Thoughts are basically electrical impulses, chemicals
and neurons. They look like a tree with branches. As the
thoughts grow and become permanent, more branches
grow and the connections become stronger.

THOUGHTS GROUPING TOGETHER LIKE TREES IN A FOREST

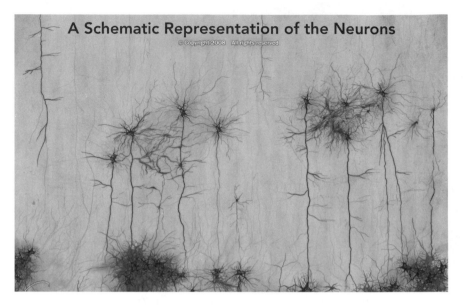

A Schematic Representation of the Neurons

As we change our thinking, some branches go away, new ones form, the strength of the connections change, and the memories network with other thoughts.[10] What an incredible capacity of the brain to change and rewire and grow! Spiritually, this is renewing the mind.

As you think, your thoughts are activated, which in turn activates your attitude, because your attitude is all of your thoughts put together and reflects your state of mind. This attitude is reflected in the chemical secretions that are released. Positive attitudes cause the secretion of the correct amount of chemicals, and negative attitudes distort the chemical secretions in a way that disrupts their natural flow. The chemicals are like little cellular signals that translate the information of your thought into a physical reality in your body and mind, creating an emotion. The combination of thoughts, emotions and resulting attitudes, impacts your body in a positive or negative way.

This means, your mind and body really are inherently linked, and this link starts with your thoughts.

The science of thought is very exciting. We have to recognize how the process can get disrupted by toxic thoughts in the brain if we're going to understand how we are negatively affected in our mental life and behavior. As we start to understand how a thought forms and impacts our emotions and bodies, we have two choices: we can let our thoughts become toxic and poisonous, or we can detox our negative thoughts, which will improve our emotional wholeness and even recover our physical health.

Does this sound familiar? "Today I have given you the choice between life and death, between blessings and curses. Now I call on heaven and earth to witness the choice you make. Oh, that you would choose life, so that you and your descendants might live!" (Deuteronomy 30:19 NLT).

You have been experiencing the affects of all your thoughts your entire life and may not have even known it! For example, have you ever become ill in the wake of a difficult or traumatic time in your life? You may not have made the connection, just chalking it up as coincidence, when it was more likely to have been the result of toxic thoughts taking their toll on your overall health.

Thoughts are not only scientifically measurable, but we can verify how they affect our bodies. We can actually feel our thoughts through our emotions.

Emotions are involved in every thought we build, ever have built and ever will build.

In fact, for every memory you make, you have a corresponding emotion attached to it, which is stored in your brain, and as a photocopy in your body's cells.

We'll look at the science of how this works more closely later, but the key is to understand that emotions are attached to thoughts. These emotions are very real and link your thoughts to the reaction in your body and mind. This is called the psychosomatic network. They can surface even years after an event has occurred, when the memory of that event is recalled.

To demonstrate how this works, take a minute to focus on an upsetting recent event in your life. As you deeply think about this event, become aware of how you are feeling and how your body is reacting to these thoughts and emotions. A cascade of chemicals is being activated by rethinking and imagining the event. The more you ponder, the stronger and more vivid this cascade becomes.

You may even start to become angry, frustrated or upset. You will start reacting to the thought mentally and physically as though it were happening all over again. What you think about expands and grows, taking on a life of its own. The direction this life takes could be positive or negative; you get to choose (Isaiah 7:15 KJV).[11] What you choose to think about can foster joy, peace and happiness or the complete opposite.

In fact, your thoughts create changes right down to genetic levels, restructuring the cell's makeup. Scientists have shown this restructuring is how diseases are able to take hold in the body. On the flip side, when we choose non-toxic thinking, we step into a whole new realm of brain and body function. "Feel good" chemicals are released that make us feel peaceful and also promote healing, memory formation and deep thinking, which increase intelligence when combined together.

Healthy, non-toxic thoughts help nurture and create a positive foundation in the neural networks of the mind.

These positive thoughts strengthen positive reaction chains and release biochemicals, such as endorphins and serotonin, from the brain's natural pharmacy. Bathed in these positive environments, intellect flourishes, and with it, mental and physical health.

> *And now, dear brothers and sisters, one final thing. Fix your thoughts on what is true, and honorable, and right, and pure, and lovely, and admirable. Think about things that are excellent and worthy of praise.*
> – Philippians 4:8 NLT

I often speak to groups about the science of thought, and several times over the years, I have been asked how the cycle of toxic thinking can be broken.

Using my two decades of brain research, I have identified the Dirty Dozen, areas for detox, based on the science of how the brain works. Because science is powerful, I want to reveal to you exactly how this process works in a way that is easy to understand. Then you will have the tools needed to detox your brain, to develop a lifestyle of freedom from your past, and to keep from sinking below your amazing potential.

For each principle, I have designed a series of Brain Sweep questions. Believe it or not, these questions provoke more than simple reflection. They are designed to take your brain through a specific sequence based on the science of thought. I researched and developed this process for my masters and Ph.D., and it has been used to help people learn, think, understand and improve their lives with great success.[12]

If you move through this process, in this sequence, you can find freedom from toxic thinking. As toxic thoughts are swept away, they will be replaced with the foundation for health and peace.

Your thoughts can sweep away stress, making you more clever, calm and in control of your emotions, or they can do just the opposite! The choice is yours. Every thought we think should be weighed carefully, because as we think so are we – "For as he hath thought in his soul, so [is] he . . ." (Proverbs 23:7 YLT).

The really good news about all of this is that detoxing your thought life is possible. You don't have to travel far to find some magic therapist or technique, and it won't cost a fortune. It begins with your thoughts and your reactions to those thoughts. The key is *you*!

You can take back control of your body and mind! It is possible to lead an emotionally-happy and physically-healthy lifestyle simply by learning to control your thought life.

2PART TWO
STRESS

3
CHAPTER
STRESS AND THE DIRTY DOZEN

Stress is the direct result of toxic thinking, and the Dirty Dozen all thrive on stress. The kind of stress that feeds the appetite of the Dirty Dozen is more than an increased heart rate or an uneasy feeling; rather, it is the medical definition for severe strain on your body's systems, including the brain.

So you can understand the handiwork of the Dirty Dozen more clearly, let's look at how stress really affects us.

When you are under extreme stress, chemicals flood your body and create physical effects caused by intense feelings. When those feelings are, for example, anger, fear, anxiety or bitterness, the effects on your health are nothing short of horrific in the long term.

Stress chemicals can be the kind of guests that don't know when they have overstayed their welcome. If they stay, because your system is imbalanced from toxic thinking, eventually they will tunnel deep inside the recesses of your mind, literally becoming part of who you are. Buried feelings of anger, fear, anxiety and bitterness create volcanic build-ups in your body. When you internalize wounded emotions, you allow a seething mix of anger, hostility and resentment to develop.

For this reason, hostility and rage are at the top of the list of toxic emotions; they can produce real physiological reactions in the body and cause serious mental and physical illness.

Neuroscientists can now track the sequence of reactions through which toxic thoughts, like the Dirty Dozen, carve a harmful path of destruction in your body.[1] But it's not only modern-day scientists who have known about the perils to our health from emotionally burying our heads in the sand. The biblical reference "my people are destroyed for lack of knowledge" (Hosea 4:6) demonstrates ancient wisdom and insight about this toxic pathway. Quite simply, knowledge and understanding give you the tools you need to sweep away toxic thoughts and emotions.

SCHEMATIC REPRESENTATION OF BRANCHES (DENDRITES) THAT HOLD TOXIC OR NON-TOXIC THOUGHTS

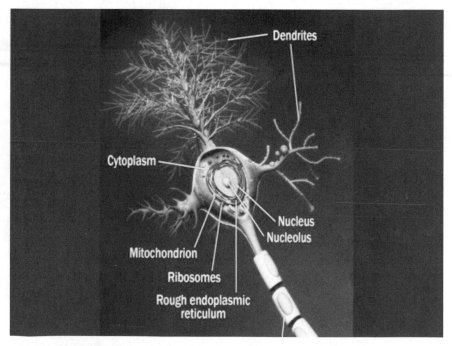

It's important to understand that two things are fundamental to your body's survival: protection and growth. Both are controlled by your brain and nervous

system.[2] The brain is like the CEO of an organization. The CEO has to grow a company and protect it from internal and external threats, or the company (in this case, your body) will have major problems.

Obviously, growth is very important for survival for many reasons. Billions of cells in your body wear out and need to be replaced every day. The lining of the intestines, for example, wears out every 72 hours.[3]

In addition to growth systems, the body has two systems that involve protection. One, the immune system, fights internal threats. The other, the Hypothalamus-Pituitary-Adrenal (HPA) axis, protects against external threats.[4]

It is also important to note that the patterns for adulthood are laid down in childhood, so an excessively stressed child could be prone to lifelong stress-related illnesses.[5]

These systems are so important in understanding stress, because if your thought life becomes toxic, your growth and protection functions will be at odds with each other. You can't have optimal growth and protection at the same time because your body usually concentrates on one or the other at any given time.[6]

Obviously, if your body spends energy and resources fighting against itself in proportion to the perceived threat or stressor, it is a drain on your energy. Ideally, your body should be focusing more on growth than protection.[7]

An illustration of when your system is out of balance is when your immune system becomes compromised. You may not know that your immune system kills most cancer cells. When cancer cells float around in your body, mighty little soldiers from your immune system destroy them – most of the time. If you are intensely worried, depressed, anxious or angry and constantly thinking of the event or person who caused you to be in that state, you can make stressors (or toxic thoughts) become stronger.

These stressors put your body into a stressful state because, as you already know, stress causes the wrong quantities of chemicals to be released. These chemicals flow through the body and can distort the DNA of the immune cells, which can make them less effective in killing the cancer cells.[8] This is an extreme example of the relationship among your thought life, stress and your immune system.

Now, it is important to understand that not all cancer is caused by stress. Our body is amazingly resistant to diseases, but under strain, it simply cannot function at its peak capabilities and becomes vulnerable to all kinds of problems.

Another example of strain on your body's protective system is an imbalance of cortisol levels. Cortisol regulates and supports functions in your heart, immune system and metabolism. However, when the cortisol level increases because of stress and flows in excess quantities through the brain, it causes memories to temporarily shrink, so you are unable to access particular memories. Have you ever taken an exam and gone completely blank? Then, when you calmed down and your systems returned to normal, you suddenly remembered all that you had studied? This happened because the stress chemicals subsided and the memories literally plumped up, giving you access to them again.[9]

Once your body is truly in stress mode and the cortisol is flowing, dendrites (which send and receive electrochemical impulses) start shrinking and even "falling off." The chemical balance in your brain goes haywire.

A Neuron (A Thought)

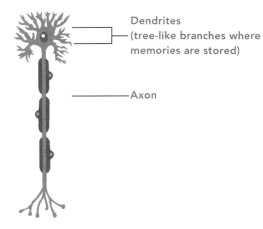

Dendrites
(tree-like branches where
memories are stored)

Axon

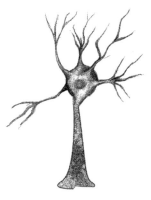

Dendrites (branches)
grow extensively on the
nerve cell as we think.

Dendrites (branches)
can shrink and fall off
with continued high
levels of stress.

Typical problems may include:

- Depression
- Phobias
- Panic attacks
- Fatigue
- Lethargy
- Exhaustion
- Insomnia
- Anxiety
- Confusion
- Lack of creativity
- Headaches and migraine headaches – which are vascular in origin, from dilation of blood vessels in the brain.
- Forgetfulness

There is a huge body of scientific research on this topic supporting the importance of dealing with your thought life when it comes to stress.[10] But the Bible is the greatest resource, telling us repeatedly not to worry and not to be afraid or anxious.

The affects of stress may seem overwhelming, but don't be discouraged because it really is possible to switch on your brain, detox and de-stress!

Toxic Emotions

Toxic emotions and toxic thoughts are a natural combination, so when you sweep away toxic thinking, toxic emotions will be swept away too!

If your thought life is toxic, you have toxic memories physically built into the nerve networks of your mind.[11]

A WELL-DEVELOPED TOXIC THOUGHT: A SCHEMATIC REPRESENTATION

A WELL-DEVELOPED HEALTHY THOUGHT: A SCHEMATIC REPRESENTATION

CHANGES IN THOUGHTS ON A CELLULAR LEVEL

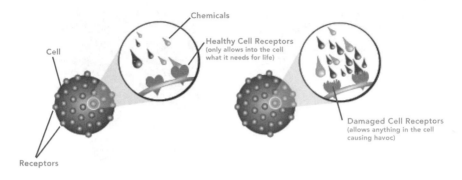

The chemicals that accompany those toxic thoughts course through your body in a myriad of toxic chain reactions. These toxic thoughts can even look distorted compared to healthy thoughts – chemicals released can change the shape and even destroy parts of the neurons, causing change right down to the cellular level.

We don't have to stay in this place of mental and physical distress caused by toxic thinking. That is exactly why I have written this book – so you can learn how to recognize and banish the Dirty Dozen.

Stress is harmful when it is sparked by negative emotions. But your body is designed to cope with brief bursts of stress like unforeseen circumstances or incredible obstacles, for example. When your system is stimulated by healthy, non-toxic thoughts, it can be very constructive; it makes you alert and focused and ready to move forward. These short bursts of stress can be protective, helping you avoid danger or preparing your brain to build helpful memories.

Stress only becomes a serious problem when it moves past the temporary stage or is sparked by toxic negative thoughts. These negative thoughts are fear driven. In fact, research shows that fear triggers more than 1,400 known physical and chemical responses. This activates more than 30 different hormones and neurotransmitters combined, throwing the body into a frantic state.[12]

4
CHAPTER
THE TOXIC PATHWAY

We live in a fast-paced world full of stressful circumstances and emotions. But we can control how stress affects us. When we break the cycle of toxic thinking, we can also break the habit of absorbing stress.

There are three stages of stress. The first stage is temporary stress. This is the sweaty palms, fast heart beat, "I have to give a presentation" kind of stress.

Then there is stage two of stress. This is when temporary stress is not released after the initial short burst and starts becoming harmful to your system.

Stage three is chronic stress. When you are in chronic stress, your systems reach exhaustion from the constant state of heightened alert.

These stages of stress are scientifically significant because they illustrate how a single toxic thought causes extreme reactions in so many of our systems.

There are consequences that can come from allowing stress to become ingrained in the "trees" of your mind.

You must confront repressed unforgiveness, anger, rage, hatred or any other form of toxic thinking. You have a medical need to forgive others and you also must forgive yourself.

Let's look closely at three systems that are particularly affected by stages two and three of stress: the heart, the immune system and the digestive system. Being aware of the toxic pathway of stress, which targets various organs and systems along the way, is important. Let's start with that very vital muscle and organ, the heart.

The Heart

Neurologically, your heart is sensitive to what you think and feel.[13] Your thoughts directly affect your heart.

Here are some examples of various heart conditions where stress is a major contributor:

- Hypertension – high blood pressure.
- Angina – chest pain and spasms of heart tissue.
- Coronary artery disease – hardening of the arteries causing narrowing, which can be triggered by anger.
- Strokes or cerebrovascular insufficiency – clogging of blood vessels so brain tissue becomes starved.
- Aneurysm – ballooning or swelling of a blood vessel on the artery or rupturing of blood vessels.

Toxic stress is particularly powerful because your heart is not just a pump. It is actually like another brain (and you thought you only had one brain!). Science demonstrates that your heart has its own independent nervous system, which is a complex system referred to as the "brain in the heart."

There are at least 40,000 neurons (nerve cells) in the heart [14] – as many as are found in various parts of the brain. In effect, the brain in your heart acts like a checking station for all the emotions generated by the flow of chemicals created by thoughts. It is proving to be a real intelligent force behind the intuitive thoughts and feelings you experience. The heart also produces an important biochemical substance called an atrial peptide (specifically ANF). It is the balance hormone that regulates many of your brain's functions and stimulates behavior.[15]

New scientific evidence on the heart's neurological sensitivity indicates there are lines of communication between the brain and the heart that check the accuracy and integrity of your thought life. The reality is, your heart is in constant communication with your brain and the rest of your body. The signals your heart sends to your brain influence not just perception and emotional processing, but higher cognitive functions as well.

The Immune System

Resentment, bitterness, lack of forgiveness and self-hatred are just a few of the toxic thoughts and emotions that can also trigger immune system disorders.[16]

When it is allowed to do so, the immune system is an army that protects you from illness and disease in your body and mind. But toxic thoughts and emotions prevent your immune system from doing what it was designed to do naturally.

Your immune system secretes peptides, or hormones, including endorphins (also called the "feel good" hormones). It sends information to the brain via immuno-peptides and receives information from the brain via neuro-peptides, so there is a direct communication between those thoughts and emotions in your thought trees and the way your immune system functions.[17]

Your immune system is definitively shown to be neurologically sensitive to your thought life. When your immune system faces an attack, such as when your thought life is toxic, it generates blood proteins called cytokines, which are known to produce fatigue and depression. In this way, toxic thoughts and the emotions they generate interfere with the body's natural healing processes. They compound the effects of illness and disease by adding new negative biochemical processes that the body must struggle to overcome.[18]

Let's look more closely at the body's autoimmune response (the immune system's response against the body's own cells). When your body faces toxic thoughts and emotions, it cannot discern its true enemy and attacks healthy cells and tissue, losing its ability to fight the true invaders.

A sudden burst of stress lowers immunity (one way to "catch a cold"). However, even more ominous is the effect of small amounts of day-to-day stress. This confuses your immune system, effectively setting in motion the autoimmune response that causes your body to turn on itself.

The Digestive System

Your digestive (or gastrointestinal) system is as important as all the other bodily systems, and it is unfortunately just as susceptible to come under attack along the Dirty Dozen's toxic pathway. Its normal function is to digest what you put into your mouth. Under normal conditions, it works hard to help you get as many nutrients as possible from everything you eat and drink, to fire up all your bodily processes and keep your organs in excellent health.

A lot of research is available on how food affects your mood. Scientists at the Massachusetts Institute of Technology were among the first to document this. Many others, including researchers at Harvard Medical School, have followed suit. For example, scientists call carbohydrates – found in pasta, breads and sweets – "comfort foods" because they boost the powerful brain chemical, serotonin, which is involved in feelings of contentment. But the comfort won't last long. Within 20 minutes of eating processed carbohydrates, any benefits will dissipate.[19]

There is also evidence showing that your thoughts and emotions can render even the best of comfort foods toxic to your body, thanks to the now undeniable link between your body and your mind. It's why dieticians and nutritionists tell you (or should tell you) never to eat when you are angry. It's almost as if the anger seeps into the food you eat, as your body tries to digest it.

You are aware by now the amount of stress chemicals your toxic thoughts and emotions release. When they are allowed to run riot in your digestive system, they create a poisonous cocktail that damages your health.

Some digestive disorders which can originate from the effects of toxic thoughts and emotions include[20]:

- Constipation
- Diarrhea
- Nausea and vomiting
- Cramping
- Ulcers
- Leaky gut syndrome – when nutrients leak out of your stomach and colon walls, and don't make it to your cells.
- Irritable bowel syndrome (spastic colon) – when the intestines either squeeze too hard or not hard enough, reducing optimum absorption of nutrients.

That's all the bad news, but there is good news and lots of it. Science clearly demonstrates the link between your thoughts and emotions, and your physical and mental well-being. The more you manage your thought life and emotions, the more you will learn to listen to your thoughts and deal constructively with them, and the more educated, balanced and life-giving your emotions will become.

Making your thoughts life-giving, not life-threatening, means you will be far less likely to suffer sickness and disease.

You can detox, sweeping the Dirty Dozen from your brain!

3 PART THREE
THE SCIENCE OF THOUGHT

If you have been told that you are doomed to repeat the patterns in your family, that you are controlled by biology, that you cannot transcend the influence of your environment, then you have been lied to and need to hear the truth.

Even if you are consumed with toxic memories, even if you live in a toxic environment that is discouraging, you can literally detoxify your thought life. You can break the chains that have been limiting your development into who God created you to be. Our brain is truly incredible; it can be re-shaped and re-formed.

Detoxifying your thoughts can be like selecting a book from a shelf in your library of memories, rewriting a page in that book, then placing it back on the shelf, free of toxic thoughts and emotions. If it happens to be a life-threatening book, you may want to do even more work on it and even get rid of the book altogether. That is part of the process of building a new, healthy thought over an old, toxic one and removing the negative emotional sting at the same time. The good news is we can change those pathways within four days and create new ones within twenty-one days![1]

In fact as soon as you are conscious of the memory, it will start changing physically in your brain.[2]

Thoughts can be measured, they occupy space, they change and grow and shrink and adapt, but most importantly, they represent you.

So it's time to ask yourself: Are your thoughts toxic? Are you toxic?

"Let all bitterness and indignation and wrath (passion, rage, bad temper) and resentment (anger, animosity) and quarreling (brawling, clamor, contention) and slander (evil-speaking, abusive or blasphemous language) be banished from you, with all malice (spite, ill will, or baseness of any kind)" (Ephesians 4:31 Amp.).

The Brain Sweep questions in Part Four will help you sweep away toxic thoughts and emotions in twelve areas of your life, taking your brain through a specific sequence designed to work with how your brain is wired. This will create lasting change, not temporary relief.

Positive habits and negative habits are built through the exact same process in your brain. The only difference is that the thoughts release different quantities of chemicals. Depending upon which kind of thought it is, either positive or negative, it will have a different structure caused by these chemicals.[3]

To detox our thought life, we must take a toxic thought back through the sequence to re-build it, or better still, learn how to avoid building it in the first place! What is the sequence? Well, to make complicated science simple, I have labeled each stage of the sequence: gather, reflect, journal, revisit and reach. These five points are a part of what I call the Switch On Your Brain™ process.[4]

This is the brain sequence I have been developing for many years in my research and clinical experience to help people think and learn for lasting success. The Brain Sweep questions trigger this process, sweeping away each area of toxic thinking, the Dirty Dozen.[5]

Although the Brain Sweep questions automatically trigger the gather, reflect, journal, revisit and reach stages, which help bring order to your library of memories, it is important to understand why they work. As the wise proverb writer says, "Also, without knowledge the soul [is] not good . . ." (Proverbs 19:2 YLT).

That's why when I share my research about toxic thinking, I always get so excited to teach about brain science – one of my favorite things! I try to make complex scientific processes come alive so everyone can understand and can learn just enough information to help detox their negative thoughts. Yes, even if you are not a science fan!

I love the science of thought because is it so freeing and, when it comes to brain science, cutting edge. Remember, science is here to help us see and understand how gracious and incredible God is.

As we think, the brain has the ability to change itself for better or for worse. The recognition of this is a gigantic and significant leap in the history of mankind.

5
CHAPTER
GATHER

As you are reading, perhaps you have some classical music playing in the background. You might be sitting in a comfortable chair, smelling the freshly-mowed lawn through an open window and savoring a piece of fruit. If you were in this idyllic setting, all five of your senses – sight, sound, smell, touch and taste – would be your contact between the external world and your internal world, activating your mind.

THE DOORWAY

As the electrical information from your five senses pours into your brain, your brain is gathering electrical impulses through your peripheral nerves (the lines of communication between your brain and your body). These senses become the doorway into your intellect, influencing your free will and your emotions.

The Dirty Dozen thrive in the dark, so understanding how electrical impulses from your five senses can turn into dangerous toxic thoughts is important. The first step in the process of forming a thought, gathering these electrical impulses, makes sense of the information coming from your five senses.

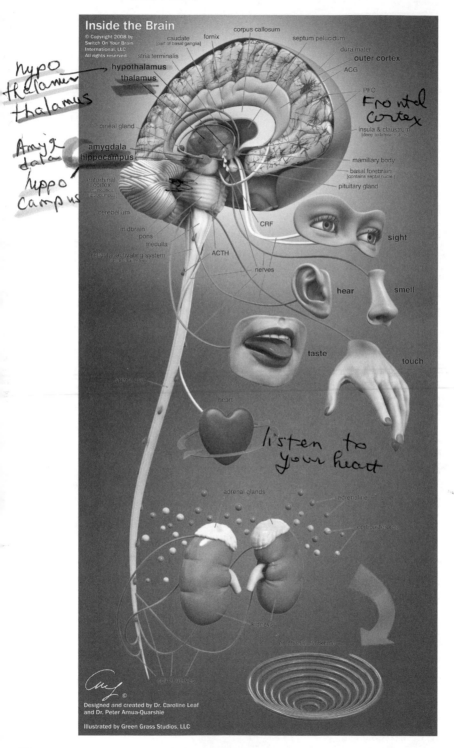

This incoming information then travels through some astonishing brain structures that flavor, enrich and distribute the information all along the way. The information is taken to a place where you can decide on the permanence of that information and whether it becomes part of who you are.

The most exciting facts of this journey are the brain's ability to react to toxic versus non-toxic information and the many opportunities we have to accept or reject incoming information. You can control the incoming information and get rid of what you don't want before it wires into your brain and affects who you are.

The days of being a victim of what the world throws at you through your five senses are about to end.[6]

THE TRANSMITTER STATION AND "BREEZE THROUGH THE TREES"

Once the information has entered your brain through any or all of your five senses, it passes a major transmitter station (the thalamus) that monitors and processes this information.

The thalamus is the meeting point for almost all the nerves that connect the different parts of the brain. You can think of the thalamus as an air traffic controller. There isn't a signal from your environment that does not pass through the thalamus. It connects the brain to the body and the body to the brain, and it allows the entire brain to receive a large amount of important data from the external and internal worlds all at once.

The thalamus transmits the electrical data throughout your brain, activating existing thoughts (or nerve cells) in the outer part of the brain, the cerebral cortex, to help you understand the incoming information. This activation of existing thoughts is what I call the "breeze through the trees" stage. The nerve cells in the cerebral cortex look like trees in a forest, and the activation sweeps through like a wind bringing the existing thoughts into consciousness.[7]

This wonderfully complex transmission of information through the cerebral cortex, or the "breeze through the trees," alerts and activates attitude. Attitude is a state of mind (all the thoughts on the trees) that influences our choices and what we say and do as a result of our choices.[8]

If the attitude activated in the cerebral cortex is negative, then the emotional response will naturally be a negative or stressed feeling within the depths of your mind. If the attitude is positive, the feeling will be peaceful. The truth is your attitude will be revealed no matter how much you try to hide it.

Then the activated attitude – positive or negative – is transmitted from the thalamus down to the hypothalamus.

The truth is your attitude will be revealed no matter how much you try to hide it.

THE CHEMICAL FACTORY

The hypothalamus is like a chemical factory where the thought-building processes happen and where the type and amount of chemicals released into the body are determined. The thalamus signals the hypothalamus to chemically prepare a response to your thoughts.[9]

The endocrine system is a collection of glands and organs that mostly produce and regulate your hormones. The hypothalamus is often referred to as the "brain" of the endocrine system, controlling things like thirst, hunger, body temperature and the body's response to your emotional life. The hypothalamus is like a pulsating heart responding to your emotions and thought life, greatly impacting how you function emotionally and intellectually.[10]

This means that if you are anxious or worried about something, the hypothalamus responds to this anxious and worrying attitude with a flurry of stress chemicals engaging the pituitary gland – the master gland of the endocrine system. The endocrine system secretes the hormones responsible for organizing the trillions of cells in your body to deal with any impending threats. Negative thoughts shift your body's focus to protection and reduce your ability to process and think with wisdom or grow healthy thoughts.

On the other hand, if you change your attitude and determine to apply God's excellent advice not to worry, the hypothalamus will cause the secretion of chemicals that facilitate the feeling of peace, and the rest of the brain will respond by secreting the correct "formula" of neurotransmitters (chemicals that transmit electrical impulses) for thought building and clear thinking.

Although you may not be able to control your environment all of the time, you can control how it affects your brain.

How? Well, this incoming information is still in a temporary state. It has not yet lodged itself into your memory or become a part of your spirit, which defines who you are.

You can choose to reject the presently-activated thoughts and the incoming information, or you can let the information make its way into your mind (your soul) and your spirit, eventually subsiding in your non-conscious, which dominates who you are. Even though you can't always control your circumstances, you can make fundamental choices that will help you control your reaction to your circumstances and keep toxic input out of your brain.[11]

To help us make good choices, we have the amygdala and hippocampus. The amygdala deals with the passionate, perceptual emotions attached to incoming thoughts and all the thoughts already in your head. The hippocampus deals with memory and motivation.[12]

Now, this is where you consciously step up to center stage, needing to make a decision whether or not these incoming thoughts will become part of who you are. Let's look more closely at how you control this decision.

THE LIBRARY — *storing emotional perceptions in response to thought*

The amygdala, a double almond-shaped structure located in your brain, is designed to protect you from any threat to your body and mind – such as danger or stress. It puts the passion behind the punch of memory formation by influencing the hippocampus to pay more attention to more established information. The amygdala deals with both positive love-based emotions like joy and happiness, as well as negative fear-based emotions like sadness, anger and jealousy.[13]

Even though you can't always control your circumstances, you can make fundamental choices that will help you control your reaction to your circumstances and keep toxic input out of your brain.

The thalamus (transmitter station) alerts the amygdala of any incoming information from the five senses, so the already alerted amygdala literally adds its "thumb print" to the incoming information – flavoring it with emotional spice. How does it do this?

The amygdala is like a library, storing the emotional perceptions that occur each time a thought is built. In other words, every time we build a memory, we activate emotions. The endocrine system and the brain have to release the correct chemicals (the molecules of emotion and information) necessary for building healthy or toxic memories. Because the amygdala is in constant communication with the hypothalamus (which secretes chemicals in response to your thought life), we are able to feel our body's reaction to our thoughts. These physical reactions – rapid heartbeat and adrenalin rushes – force us to decide whether to accept or reject the information based on how we feel physically.

To help us even more, the amygdala has lines of communication connected to the frontal lobe, which controls reasoning, decision-making, analyzing and strategizing – all executive-level functions. This connection enables us to balance the emotions we physically experience and allows us to react reasonably.

Here is the exciting part: we can choose at this moment to say things like, "I choose NOT to think about this issue anymore," and those temporary thoughts will disappear. The choice to not think about the thoughts will send them away; they simply fade.

But if we don't stop thinking about the issue, for either negative or positive thoughts, all the information including the awakened toxic or non-toxic attitude will flow into a sea horse-shaped structure called the hippocampus.

The hippocampus is a sort of clearing house for thoughts. It classifies incoming information as having either short or long-term importance and "files" it accordingly, converting temporary thoughts into permanent thoughts that become part of who you are (a lot of this happens at night while you are sleeping).[14]

To do this, the hippocampus needs to work with the central hub of the brain – a whole group of structures that integrate all the activated memories and work with the hippocampus to convert information into your permanent memory storage.

This is where we begin some serious reflection in order to make some life-changing decisions. Ask yourself, "Do I want this information to be a part of me or not?"

A good point to remember is toxic memories create stress and the hippocampus is extremely vulnerable to stress, as it is rich in stress hormone receptors (tiny "doorways" on cells that receive chemical information) that are normally used to reinforce memories. For these brain cells, excessive stress is like setting off a firecracker in a glass jar, causing the hippocampus to lose cells and shrink.[15] This affects the communication between the hippocampus and the central hub of the brain, keeping it from building good memories.

Let's move to the reflect stage and see how the hippocampus works with the central hub of the brain in building thoughts.

stress - prevents good memories.

6

CHAPTER
REFLECT

Reflecting is a biblical principle. If you look at Proverbs, you will see that we are instructed to gain wisdom and meditate on knowledge until we understand. If you are going to get out of any toxic thinking jam, you need to think, understand and apply the wisdom you gain.

Thankfully you have all the structures and physiological processes at your disposal to do this. Neuroscience is for your benefit and to help you enjoy every day. This means no thought should ever be allowed to control you. Becoming more self aware of negative thoughts should be your goal in this process.

Neuroscience is for your benefit and to help you enjoy every day.

After the gathering stage, electrical information created by your thoughts and existing memories brought into conscious-ness whoosh through the hippocampus, moving toward the front of the brain (the basal forebrain, which is behind the inside corners of your eyes). The information stays in the hippocampus for 24 to 48 hours constantly being amplified each time it swirls to the front.[16]

The amplification sets in motion a delightful string of events so magnificent that it can only reflect the work of our Creator. This string of events is our free will and decision-making ability, a true gift.

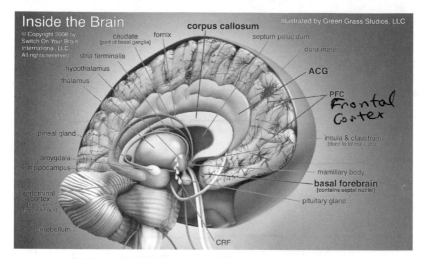

This amplification means the thought is very conscious and becomes "labile" or unstable, which means it is moldable and can be changed. In fact, it must change. The science of thought demands that change must occur – either reinforcing the thought as it is or changing some or all of it.[17]

The memory cannot sink back as part of our attitude into our non-conscious mind without being changed in some way. This is marvelous news for us but emphasizes the responsibility we need to take for our thought life. No thought is harmless, nor does it stay the same – it constantly changes.

This means the harder we think, the more change we can make. What is this change? Proteins are made and used to grow new branches to hold your thoughts, a process called protein synthesis. So, if we don't get rid of the thought we reinforce it. This is quite phenomenal because science is confirming that we can choose to interfere with protein synthesis by our free will. If you say you "can't" or "won't," this is a decision of your free will and will actually cause protein synthesis and changes in the real estate of your brain. Now "bringing into captivity every thought" (2 Corinthians 10:5 KJV) starts to become a lot more important. Thoughts are constantly remodeled by the "renewing of your mind" (Romans 12:2 NIV).

No thought is harmless, nor does it stay the same – it constantly changes.

AN ACTIVE THOUGHT: A SCHEMATIC REPRESENTATION

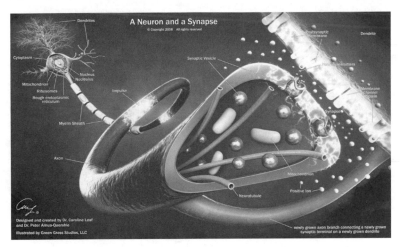

You have to make a decision: do you want to build memories out of this new information coming into your mind?

When we do this, we actually change the physical structure (called neuroplasticity) of the brain, because thinking causes really important neurotransmitters (chemicals in the brain that carry electrical impulses) to flow. These neurotransmitters – serotonin in particular – cause changes deep inside the cell, effecting genetic expression and protein synthesis, as I described earlier.

Research has shown that mental practice – imagination, visualization, deep thought and reflection – produces the same physical changes in the brain as it would physically carrying out the same imagined processes.[18]

We see this principle in the Bible, when it says that "nothing they have imagined they can do will be impossible for them" (Genesis 11:6 Amp.). Brain scans show that the same parts of the brain activated by action, are the same parts of the brain activated by simply thinking about an action. This sheds whole new depths of understanding for the scripture: "Faith is the substance of things hoped for, the evidence of things not seen" (Hebrews 11:1).

Rehearsing things mentally is a great everyday example of how we can think and more deeply reflect on daily actions, because each time we do this, we change the memory. For example, if a surgeon is about to perform an operation, he would mentally rehearse each precise step in his mind first, as would an athlete before a game or someone about to take an exam. As we mentally rehearse it even more, the newly-built memory becomes stronger and stronger and starts to grow more connections to neighboring nerve cells, integrating that thought into other thought patterns.[19]

A healthy thought and toxic thought can both be built with mental rehearsal. But we can literally tear toxic strongholds down by choosing to bring the thought into conscious awareness for analysis, and then changing it through repentance and forgiveness (causing protein synthesis) and replacing it with the correct information, using Philippians 4:8 or something similar as a guideline.

When talking about thinking, free will and understanding, we need to also consider the exciting contribution the heart makes to thinking and decision-making. Your heart is not just a pump; it helps with choices, acting like a checking station for all the emotions generated by the flow of chemicals from thoughts.

Your heart is in constant communication with your brain and the rest of your body, checking the accuracy and integrity of your thought life. As you are about to make a decision, your heart pops in a quiet word of advice, well worth listening to, because when you listen to your heart, it secretes the ANF hormone that gives you a feeling of peace.[20]

There is no such thing as a harmless thought, so we
need to be good stewards of our thoughts and emotions.

When you think deeply to understand, you go beyond
just storing facts and answers to storing key concepts and
strategies to help you come up with your own answers.[21]

These thoughts have been consolidated and stabilized
sufficiently so that you have immediate access to them.
When this happens, you have achieved a level of expertise.
This can happen in a negative or positive direction with all
the contributing effects (see Part Two).

We should aim for that which we were naturally designed
– deep intellectual non-toxic thought. Reflecting helps with
this process, but for protein synthesis to consolidate, stabilize,
and become part of you, ~~repetition and rehearsal in frequent~~,
spaced intervals is necessary. Research shows that around seven
deep thinking exercises over a period of twenty-one days help
create long-lasting change.[22] The next three stages in thought
formation – journaling, revisiting and reaching – show you
how to take advantage of these exercises to stabilize your
protein synthesis or bring your memory up again and
change it.

CHAPTER
JOURNAL

Writing down your thoughts is important in the Switch On Your Brain™ process, because the actual process of writing consolidates the memory and adds clarity to what you have been thinking about. It helps you see more clearly the areas that need detoxing, because it literally allows you to look at your brain on paper. Writing helps you see your non-conscious and conscious thoughts in a visual way.

The basal ganglia, the cerebellum and motor cortex are involved in this process, but let's talk about the basal ganglia first. (See page 50 for "Inside the Brain" diagram.)

Nestling between the cerebral cortex (on the outside of the brain) and the midbrain (in both the left and right hemi-spheres) are intricate bundles of neurological networks that are interconnected with the cerebral cortex.

These bundles are the basal ganglia. The basal ganglia also put their "fingerprint" on the process of thinking and learning by helping the hippocampus, frontal lobe and corpus callosum turn thought and emotion into immediate action.[23]

The basal ganglia do this by helping ensure the memory gets built into the trees of the cerebral cortex. They also smooth out fine motor actions and set the idle rate for anxiety. So they literally help us write down (together with the motor cortex of the brain – the cerebellum), the information we have just understood.

Now, how we write down our thoughts is really important, because some ways of writing down information are more brain-compatible than traditional linear and one-color note taking. See my DVD series, *Switch On Your Brain*™, for ideas on how to be brain-compatible when you are writing.[24]

I always encourage anyone who is keeping a thought journal to be creative with their notes. I also encourage anyone moving through the process of detoxifying thoughts to be playful with their thought journal. Don't limit yourself to just writing in straight lines.

If there are word associations or groupings that seem natural as you focus on information, group those on a page. Draw a picture or diagram to go along with that thought expression. Add color or texture.

Pour out the impressions in your mind onto a page.

When I am helping students develop their learning and retention skills, I teach them the Metacog™ method I've developed.[25] The name might seem a little odd, but the process is fascinating.

It's really simple; you group patterns that radiate from a central point. Each pattern linked to the central point creates a branch. Then you continue to develop each of the branches by linking more detailed patterns. The process can continue until you have explored every nuance of your thought.

If you are interested in an example of a Metacog™, I have included one in Appendix A.

It may seem a little strange at first, but this method of pouring out your thoughts encourages both sides of the brain to work together, integrating the two perspectives of thought – the left side of the brain looks at information from details to the big picture and the right side of the brain from the big picture to details.

For full understanding to take place, which will result in the conversion of short-term memory to long-term memory, both perspectives of thought need to come together.

Seeing your thoughts on paper and evaluating the way you think and what you are thinking about are great ways of journaling your thought patterns in order to detox your thought life.

Hypo Thalamus chemical factory
type + amt of chemicals released
happen

Thalamus - transmitter station
gets info from 5 senses

Amygdala - put it emotional
thumbprint on it.

library
connects with frontal lobe
Can choose at this point not
to have this temporary thought
permanent.

8
CHAPTER
REVISIT

Revisiting what you have written will be a revealing process. After you have considered the input from your five senses, focused on your thought, journaled about it (or created a Metacog™) – you will have stimulated major neuroplastic rewiring and your brain will be in a highly active and dynamic state. (See page 50 for "Inside the Brain" diagram.)

Earlier I spoke about when thoughts are activated and pushed into the conscious mind, they enter a labile state – meaning they can be altered. They have to be reconsolidated and new proteins made, reconfiguring their neuronal connections.[26]

They can be redesigned and changed or kept the same and reinforced.

God builds into the science of thought this amazing ability to renew our minds. This means when you think about a thought, each time the thought is dominating your conscious mind, you can do something with it. You can choose to keep it the same or change it. Either way, protein synthesis happens. The toxic memory will either be changed or strengthened. Revisiting what you have journaled and using reflection lay down new circuits and help detox the brain.

This process is the major role of the revisit stage. When a memory becomes unstable, it can be modified, toned down or retranscribed by interfering with protein synthesis, an important molecular process in thought consolidation.

Thoughts can be redesigned when they are consciously captured.

Not only do you have the opportunity to examine your thoughts on paper, but you have the opportunity to rethink through your reaction to the information – evaluating how toxic the thought is and then retranscribing it to be a healthy and strong part of your memory library.

At the end of every single one of the Dirty Dozen chapters in Part Four are a series of Brain Sweep questions. I encourage you to move through the questions in sequence, and after you have written down your thought in whatever format works best for you, ask yourself the "revisit" questions for that principle. This gives you the power to change and rewire it.

By applying these Brain Sweep questions, you are neuroplastically transcribing these memories and making the non-conscious conscious so you can see what is toxic and understand why and how it is affecting your life. Then you can change or rewire these memories. Scientifically this process is called "retranscribing neuroplastically"; spiritually this process is called "the renewing of your mind"(see Romans 12:2).

It's exciting and empowering to know that we have the mental and intellectual capacity to do this process ourselves, with the help of God's grace and His unfailing wisdom.

We have been given a divine gift – an opportunity to break free from the chains of toxic events in our past or lies we have believed about ourselves and our potential.

By consciously becoming aware of our thought lives we are retranscribing and changing our underlying neuronal networks. We need to uncover the toxic thoughts that create such powerful internal conflicts in our minds, which are capable of causing such radical electrochemical imbalances that, when taken to the extreme, cause parts of ourselves to be cut off from the rest of us. Revisiting is hugely instrumental in this retranscribing and rewiring process.

There is a major factor coming into play here: we cannot control our circumstances, but we can control our reactions to those circumstances.

In revisiting, you are not only looking at how you think about circumstances, but you are also rethinking through your reactions, evaluating the toxicity levels, and retranscribing them. This is where the Bible is great, it lays out for us all the correct management principles for toxicity. At this revisit stage, if you discover you are a worrier, the scripture in Matthew 6:25 where we are instructed to not worry about tomorrow would be a good verse for you to apply.

If you line up your revisit with the principles outlined in God's Word (instead of worldly psychology), you have a foolproof method for doing the right thing.

9
CHAPTER
REACH

This is the stage where you reach out beyond toxic thinking by applying the principle "faith without works is dead" (James 2:20). This is where your faith manifests, where you actually do something with the detoxing that has been going on till now. You reach further. It is the final step to switching on your brain and detoxing, but you should only apply it once you have been through all of the previous steps and completed the process. That way you can move forward, changed in a positive direction. You can't reach with success without the foundation created by the previous steps.

For example, this is when you really do forgive that person who treated you badly. This is when you really believe your healing will happen; or when you really do stop worrying about your children and trust they will make the right decisions because God is watching over them; when you really do confess and believe that God will provide your needs; when you really do finally lose that excess weight; when you really do discipline your mind to stop dwelling on the past; and when you refuse to talk negatively about a situation no matter how tempting it is to do so. This is when you reach beyond where you are.

Moving through the sequence (gather, reflect, journal, revisit, reach) to detox your thoughts, you will have built a secure foundation for change, health and wholeness.

It will not work, however, if you just mouth a positive confession without a solid foundation.

Building a structure for change on a faulty foundation will never create persistent patterns in your brain to bring you peace; instead, they will fall down when the proverbial wolf (trouble) blows down your house of sticks (confessions without foundation).

In the brain, building a foundation is called integrity; you are using your words and actions to line up the thought with its beliefs and feelings. Neuroscientifically it goes like this (going through the gather, reflect, journal and revisit processes that we've learned about): the amygdala provides input to the mind on the emotions; the thalamus and hypothalamus provide input on motivation; the memory networks provide information on the existing memories; the central hub in the brain mixes and integrates this all together; the heart adds its five cents to the equation; and you make the decision. (See page 50 for "Inside the Brain" diagram.)

You can be presented with all the reason, logic, scientific evidence and just plain common sense in the world, but you won't believe something is true unless your brain's limbic system (the central location of your emotions) allows you to feel that it is true. You can't imagine and feel (change your brain structurally) one way and speak something different, without a lack of integrity operating in your brain.

Reaching helps you "feel" if something is true or not. It helps you line up the thought (imagination) with the confession (words coming out your mouth) and action. Clearly then, "confess with your mouth the Lord Jesus and believe in your heart . . ." (Romans 10:9-10) becomes the principle operating here.

You can't trick yourself, and you can't trick God. After all, you are made in His image and are, therefore, exceptionally intelligent.

Finally, we need to understand a really fascinating concept about the power of thought; when we think and use our free will to make a decision, we influence which genes are initiated (expressed) in our nerve cells. This is called epigenetics (emphasizes that our perceptions of life shape our biology and not the other way around) and quite brilliantly shows us the power of our thought life, upholding the scripture: "For as he thinks in his heart, so is he" (Proverbs 23:7).

Here is a brief summary of how this works. Every cell in your body has been neatly packaged with all the genes for you, but not all those genes are initiated (expressed) at the same time. So a cell initiates the liver gene when in your liver and not when in your skin. When a gene is expressed it makes a new protein that alters the structure and function of that particular cell.

The information about how to make these proteins is "transcribed" or read from the individual gene. The myth we have learned is that our genes shape us, but research shows that our thinking also affects which genes are initiated. Therefore, we can shape our genes.[27]

This then influences the formation of long-term memory where neurons will actually change their shape and increase the number of connections they have to other nerve cells.

This means we do not have to be victims of our biology and, as we reach, we finish what we started at the input phase, reshaping the brain's microscopic anatomy. As you move through the detoxing process, you produce changes in gene expression that alter the strength of the memory and structural changes that alter the anatomy of the thought. This is a timeless success principle designed by God.

When we spend more time examining the Dirty Dozen, the Brain Sweep questions will automatically take your brain through this important sequence, bringing you freedom from toxic thoughts and emotions.

4 PART FOUR
THE DIRTY DOZEN

Now that we've learned about how important it is to break the cycle of toxic thinking, let's meet the Dirty Dozen – twelve areas of toxic thinking in our lives.

For each area of toxic thinking, there is a series of Brain Sweep questions designed to trigger a sequence of thought that will help you sweep away negative thoughts and emotions.

By applying these Brain Sweep questions you can neuroplastically retranscribe (change or rewire) these toxic memories because, once conscious, thoughts are modifiable right down to the level of genetic expression in your DNA. As you consciously think, thoughts become unstable and have to be altered in either a positive or negative direction; they never stay the same. Even if you don't change the content of the thought, it will still retranscribe through protein synthesis, making new proteins to strengthen the thought. The bad thought can get worse, or the good thought can get better – no thought stays neutral.[1]

Scientifically this process is called "retranscribing neuroplastically." You may be familiar with the spiritual aspect of this process, the "renewing of your mind" (Romans 12:2).

You can expect definite "brain change" within 21 days – if you work consciously and intensively at least seven to twelve times a day. You may choose to concentrate on just one area of toxic thinking at a time, or you may choose to dive into all twelve for a three-week journey of breaking the cycle of toxic thinking.[2]

Before you begin to sweep away toxic thoughts and memories, here are some helpful tips:

1. Be honest with yourself and with God. Remember, God created you uniquely. Since He knows all things, He won't be shocked (see Psalm 51:6).

2. Change will happen in your brain as soon as you start the process. Within four days you will feel the effects of changed thinking; within 21 days you will have built a whole new thought pattern, literally, a new circuit in your brain.

3. Though change begins immediately, the entire process takes time to complete. Because it is a process and you are working on renewing your mind, breaking toxic thinking is ongoing.

4. The first four days will be the most difficult. The 5th-21st days will become easier as you progress. By the 21st day, you will feel a marked change.

5. Even though you'll feel a significant change after 21 days, you will need to still be mindful of practicing your new thought pattern. Repeated practice will help you develop a habit of building new and healthy thoughts and memories.

6. Remember the Apostle Paul advocates leaving the past behind (Philippians 3:13). You are not chained to your past or even your present. You can choose to be free from toxic thoughts and memories and step forward into your future.

10
CHAPTER
TOXIC THOUGHTS

Of the Dirty Dozen, Toxic Thoughts is probably the easiest to throw out before it takes hold and becomes a permanent resident of your mind.

So far, we've learned how a thought forms and how toxic thinking affects us, keeping in mind that if our thoughts are powerful enough to make us sick, they are powerful enough to help calm our minds, as well. Now let's see how we can catch Toxic Thoughts before they become part of who we are.

Remember, our behavior follows our thoughts, not the other way around. Analyzing and addressing our thoughts are key components of conquering the habits and behaviors that seem to hold us hostage. Some of us may have common symptoms of toxic thinking such as pride, anger, rebellion, self-pity, complaining and ungratefulness, while other symptoms can be as dramatic as compulsive gambling, criticizing, overeating or viewing pornography.

The actual physical change detoxing creates in our thought lives can unlock the mentally-imposed chains that bind us to our compulsive behaviors and the unsatisfactory circumstances we may find ourselves in.

So, let's capture those thoughts!

Brain Sweep

GATHER

- When you are thinking about your thought life and *gathering* information, what are your five senses telling you? Are there any toxic memories or thoughts that cross your mind, even fleetingly?
- Are you *gathering* a lot of toxic could-haves, would-haves and if-onlys?
- Are you *gathering* memories of conversations on repeat in your mind? Speculations?
- Are you *gathering* passivity? Dishonesty? Distorted thinking? False perceptions?
- Are you *gathering* a personal identity from a problem or disease?
- Are you *gathering* mayhem — one thought tumbling undeterred over another?

REFLECT

- Now *reflect*, "What am I thinking about?" Take a moment to answer yourself.
- Try to focus on each thought. How many complete thoughts are you thinking? How many half thoughts are running through your mind?
- Is there a particular thought that keeps rearing its head? This might be a habit or a pattern.
- Next, start discussing with yourself, prayerfully, the actual content of the thought that you've brought into your conscious mind. Become very aware of all that you are thinking.

JOURNAL

- Now, pour out your thoughts onto paper. As you *journal* or Metacog™, do you notice any patterns? Do you notice words or images that repeatedly come to mind?

REVISIT

- Be honest with yourself. Start sorting through your thoughts, adding, changing, evaluating. Think about what you have written down.
- As you *revisit* what you have written, ask yourself, "Does this line up with Scripture? Does this line up with what God has promised? Do I have any responsibility in this? Who do I need to forgive? Do I need to forgive myself?" Add this to your journal entry, comparing what has brought you pain with what you know to be true in God's Word.
- Write the resolution you would like to see and pray about the situation, that God would heal this area of your life and the life of anyone involved. In your journal entry, write your dreams for love, pour out your heart to God.
- Maybe talk it through with someone you trust, who can give you wise advice.

REACH

- Now it's time to *reach* beyond the Toxic Thoughts and bring health and life to your mind. This is where you step out in faith and really start to practice the changes you want to make in your life and thoughts.
- This is the time for God's Word to come alive in your life. Make a decision to forgive. What steps can you take to move beyond the pain of the past and move into your future? What steps can you take to catch Toxic Thoughts before they take hold? Is it turning off that negative TV program? Is it choosing to believe what God says about you in His Word, rather than the harmful words someone directed your way? For example, if the main area of toxicity currently in your life is worry, you can stop yourself each time it starts and confess a favorite do-not-worry scripture over the situation.
- As you *reach*, ask yourself, "How can I catch negative thoughts and sweep them away before they become a part of me?"

CHAPTER
TOXIC EMOTIONS

Are your emotions toxic? Are they making you toxic?

This member of the Dirty Dozen, Toxic Emotions, counts on the fact that emotions and thoughts are intertwined and inseparable.

It is not just your brain that stores memory; your body also holds memories in its cells. Because of this cellular memory and the communication between the cells of your body and brain, if your brain interprets incoming information as worry or depression, then every immune cell of your body will receive that interpretation instantly. This is known as the mind-body link.[3]

Suppressing, repressing or denying emotions blocks the flow of the vital, feel-good, unifying chemicals running our biology and behavior.

There are only two types of emotions, each with their own anatomy and physiology: love and fear. All other emotions are variations of these. Out of the love branch come emotions of joy, trust, caring, peace, contentment, patience, kindness, gentleness, etc. Fear-based emotions include bitterness, anger, hatred, rage, anxiety, guilt, shame, inadequacy, depression, confusion, etc.

These emotions directly affect our bodies because the amount of chemicals released is based on which group the emotions belong to – either the love-based or fear-based group. Obviously, weeding out emotions based on fear will greatly detoxify your thought life. In fact, researchers have even identified a neural circuit for holding learned fear in check.

When we experience love emotions, our brains and bodies function differently – better actually – than if we experience fear emotions. The <u>negative, fear-based emotions force the body into backup systems just to hold the fear in check,</u> which is not the ideal and not the first choice. Science and the Bible teach us not to fear!

The fact is, although you are completely unaware of the mechanisms by which it happens, thought formation and emotional expression are always tied to a specific flow of chemicals in your body. If you chronically suppress emotions, you de-stabilize and disturb the intricate psychosomatic network by interfering with the peptide flow and reaction chains. This has a negative impact on emotions and intellect.

In a nutshell, emotions bring the whole body into a single purpose, integrating systems and coordinating mental processes and biology to create behavior. Keeping the reaction chains working well is the key to controlling Toxic Thoughts, Toxic Emotions and toxic bodies, unleashing your gift.

Have you ever thrown a whole lot of clutter into a closet just before guests arrived, only to hear a loud noise as the closet door suddenly opened and everything fell out in full view of your guests? The same thing can happen in your emotional life. If you repress and hide toxic emotions, the time will surely come when those buried emotions will suddenly come pouring out. And, of course, it will happen at the most inopportune time, because buried emotions are not controlled, thoughtful emotions.

When you block emotions for years, you become an expert at not feeling what you feel, because you have neuroplastically built a pathway that says, "I will not allow myself to feel." Many people do exactly the same thing. The next steps start revealing this problem by making you look inside yourself to bring back the balance.

Let's get those emotions under control! Remember, as you go through these questions, a sequence will be triggered in your brain for lasting change. There is hope, and you really can get rid of those Toxic Emotions!

 **Brain Sweep**

GATHER

- The thoughts you build have emotions attached to them.
- As your brain is *gathering* thoughts, ask yourself, what attitude or state of mind (all your thoughts with their emotions attached) is influencing your choices and behavior?

REFLECT

- As you *reflect* on your emotions, think about the experiences or memories that may be causing those emotions. Are they happy memories that bring you joy? Are they hurtful memories that drag up unhappiness from your past?
- Take a moment now to examine your emotions and ask yourself, "How can I describe the emotions I am feeling?" As you focus just on your emotions, not your thoughts, can you put them into words? Your emotions will guide you a lot here, because your feelings are the emotions attached to the thoughts. A peaceful feeling reflects a

healthy thought, while a disturbed feeling reflects a toxic thought.

JOURNAL

- Now pour out your thoughts onto paper. As you *journal* or Metacog™, do you notice any patterns? Do you notice words or images repeatedly coming to mind?
- This *journaling* step tends to reveal the clutter in your closet, because the Metacog™ draws the unconscious into the conscious. Allow your cluttered emotions to pour out onto your Metacog™, rather than at the next dinner party.

REVISIT

- As you *revisit* what you have written, ask yourself, "Are there signs of suppressed emotions (besides illness in your body) like irritability, short temper, over-reaction, over-sensitivity, anxiety, frustration, fear, impulsiveness, desire for control, perfectionism or self-doubt?"
- Are there signs of imbalance between emotion and reason in your life or a situation you are facing?

REACH

- Expressing emotions is an important step in detoxing the brain.
- You don't have to "wear your heart on your sleeve" or let everything "hang out." You just need to express emotions appropriately, in a safe, accepting and non-judgmental environment.
- Don't deny your feelings. Acknowledge them, face them, and deal with them in a positive way as soon as you can. Remember, don't overindulge your emotions – adopt a policy of *admit it, quit it and beat it.*
- Ask yourself specific ways you can *reach* beyond what is holding you back. Are there steps you can take starting right now? Prayerfully put these steps into action.

12
CHAPTER
TOXIC WORDS

Toxic Words is a sneaky member of the Dirty Dozen. No discussion of thoughts and their impact on your health would be complete without examining the words that arise out of your thoughts.

Words are the symbolic output of the exceptional processes happening on microanatomical, epigenetic and genetic levels in the brain. The words you speak are electromagnetic life forces that come from thoughts inside your brain. They are influenced by your five senses and result from choices you have made. They reflect your attitude.

They contain power and work hand-in-hand with your thought life, influencing the world around you and the circumstances of your life.

I am talking about much more than just positive thinking – framing your world with words is not just about talking positively.

Your words have to be backed up with honesty, what the science of thought calls integrity (see Part Two). What you do and say on the outside must reflect what you think on the inside. A lack of integrity causes stress and affects the way information is processed and memories (thoughts) are built.

Remember, we are to account for every idle word we speak, as our words affect not only us, but those who hear us.[4] This principle is found in both Scripture and science. Words kill or give life; they're either poison or fruit – you choose (see Proverbs 18:21).

Let's sweep away those Toxic Words and grow life-giving words!

 **Brain Sweep**

GATHER
- As you think about the words you speak, or maybe the words that have been spoken about you, notice what thoughts you are *gathering*. Are there any toxic memories or thoughts that even fleetingly cross your mind?
- What input is moving from your unconscious store of thoughts into your conscious mind and is about to pop out your mouth right at this moment?

REFLECT
- Now *reflect* on what is in your conscious mind. Don't speak; just ask and answer, silently discussing the following questions with yourself: "Are my thoughts positive? Is this someone else's beliefs or words that I am just blindly agreeing with? Is it wisdom?"
- What is my objective in saying this? When I sow these words, what harvest will I reap?
- If I were to put my thoughts into words, would I regret my words?

JOURNAL
- Now pour out your thoughts onto paper. As you *journal* or Metacog™, notice any patterns, repeated words or images coming to mind.

- As part of training yourself in this detox principle of watching your words, it's great to use the Metacog™ to write down what you want to say. When you see your words on paper and the attitude that brought them about, you will see the impact your words have on others and yourself.
- The Metacog™ will draw out of you the reason for your words. The true you will surface. You may not like what's there, but it would be preferable for those thoughts to be captured in the Metacog™, which you can throw away, rather than spoken into someone else's life or your own.
- You are the "input" in someone else's life. Make sure your input is one to be proud of; we're responsible for the impact we have on others. We need to increase our awareness of the input we have in others' lives.

REVISIT
- Look at what you have written. Replace the negative with positive. If you are at a place where you have been hurt and are battling to release the poison in you, remind yourself that God will answer the prayers you want answered if you get rid of your poisonous words.
- Like poison ivy, words have their sting. You may think you'll feel better when you've let it all out and given others a "piece of your mind," but you actually won't. The science of thought and the Word of God are very clear that nothing good comes out of negative words.
- Negative words can be more harmful to you than the person you say them to, because your mind formed the toxic thought, meditated on the words and spoke them – reinforcing them in your mind. Because you created a negative stronghold, your body reacts with stress. If the stress chemicals flow in your brain for longer than 30 seconds, your thinking, intelligence, body and everything else are all going to be negatively affected.

- You can take what could be a negative situation, for you and for those who would hear your toxic words, and turn it into a positive situation by rechecking your motives, attitudes and choice of words.

REACH

- When you speak use the wisdom God has revealed to you through this process! *Reach* beyond negative patterns and bring life with your words. What areas in your life could be positively affected when you choose your words wisely?
- If you do slip, which we all do, never despair, just walk through the process again. When you repent and forgive yourself, let God help work out the best way of repairing the damage. Apologizing is a humbling experience, but one that is good for our character.

13
CHAPTER
TOXIC CHOICES

Are you making Toxic Choices over healthy choices?
Toxic Choices, a leader in the Dirty Dozen, can linger
in our minds and our lives, causing us to experience
emotions like regret, doubt and unforgiveness.

Each of the choices we make concerning our thoughts,
emotions, words and behavior, has consequences.

God gave us the gift of choice – this is a Scriptural and
scientific fact.

The new science of epigenetics (which teaches that
our perceptions and life experiences remodel our genes,
not the other way around) has changed the conventional
understanding of genetic control. It argues against the
central dogma that genes control everything, including
behavior and emotions. This means we are not, nor have
we ever, been the victims of our biology.[5]

The implications of this are obvious: we need to take
responsibility for our choices and subsequent words,
actions and behavior. We can't blame anyone else. The
science behind how a thought forms runs alongside the
science of epigenetics. What is common to both is that
genes are inside the DNA, which is inside the nucleus
of the cell. The genes code for proteins, and proteins
are the building blocks of life.

"I call heaven and earth as witnesses today against you, that I have set before you life and death, blessing and cursing; therefore choose life, that both you and your descendants may live . . ." (Deuteronomy 30:19).

Genetic expression means proteins are made according to the genetic code. But here is the exciting part, when it comes to emotions, memories and behaviors, science tells us genes are switched on and off by an external source, such as thoughts, from the environment outside the cell.[6]

The thoughts we think switch our genes on, causing genetic expression and making proteins synthesize and memories grow. You can switch your behavioral and emotional genes on and off with the choices you make. The choices of your free will, quite literally, flip the switch for memory building.

This is why it is critically important that we desire to know God's thoughts through His Word. We can make choices that bring life, not death.

Let's walk through the process of building a foundation for wise choices!

Brain Sweep

GATHER
- Start by *gathering* an awareness of how past experiences and conditioning, attitudes and habits may have influenced some of the choices you have made.

REFLECT
- Now prayerfully discuss with God these past experiences and habits that may have formed. One at a time, focus on

how they have influenced the choices you have made and the choices you are making. Discuss whether these choices were life or death choices and why.

- Train yourself to slow down and consider all the options when making choices; it's a disciplined process.

JOURNAL

- Again, pour out your thoughts onto paper. As you *journal* or Metacog™, do you notice any patterns? Do you notice words or images that repeatedly come to mind?
- Write these present and past choices down with all the discussions that came up in the reflect step above.
- Remember, although all these steps are broken down separately, they will cross over each other.

REVISIT

- Look at the choices you have made in the past.
- How do they compare to the choices you are making now?
- Add in the consequences and results of the choices you have made and are making.
- Are there patterns in them that will reflect your conditioning and habits and attitudes?
- This will reveal what needs changing and how you are making choices. You will learn much, especially if you constantly refer to the wisdom of the Word of God as you work through this process.

REACH

- How can you apply what you have learned to the new choices you make today and during the rest of your life?
- This is ongoing – you may not be a perfect decision-maker yet, but you can keep on improving.

14
CHAPTER
TOXIC DREAMS

This member of the Dirty Dozen waits patiently for nightfall to reveal himself. The good news is that we can learn from what is revealed in our dreams, especially toxic ones.

Detoxing the brain doesn't just take place when you are awake. When you are dreaming, different parts of your body and mind are exchanging information, and your glial cells (support cells in the brain) are cleaning up your memory networks, preparing for the next day. Any poorly-built memories are cleaned up while you dream.

Even more exciting is that many studies show the level of sleep we must achieve in order to dream helps the memories we build become physically stronger and more solid. If you learn something during the day, the next day, after a good night's sleep, you will have better understanding. So, "sleeping on the problem" is a good thing.[7]

People often tell me they can't remember their dreams or they never dream. The truth is, we all dream; it's a psychological process. Many of us simply suppress our dreams because of the emotions they evoke, or we simply forget them.

Our dreams challenge us to sort out our emotional lives. The more turbulent and disturbing your dreams, the more work you have to do on your thought life.

Strong emotions that are not processed thoroughly are stored on the cellular level. At night, or whenever you dream, stored information releases and bubbles up into consciousness as a dream. The content of your dreams reaches your awareness as stories, complete with plot and characters drawn in the language of your everyday awareness, though not always in a way you may immediately understand.

In fact, dreams often feel strange because during the day we process from concrete to abstract, while at night, we process the other way around – from abstract to concrete. There is a kind of "thinking" behind dreams, but as abstract ideas, visually represented and confusing. Furthermore, because of the biochemicals of emotion, dreams not only have content but feelings as well.[8]

On a physiological level, your dream state allows the psychosomatic network to retune itself and get ready for the demands of your waking life. Shifts occur in your brain's reaction chains, as chemicals spill out into the system and bind to receptors, causing activities necessary for homeostasis (balance). Then information about these readjustments enters consciousness in the form of a dream.

God is so concerned about us that He will help us sort our lives out even as we sleep. Brain scans show us that when we dream, the part of the brain that processes emotional perceptions, the amygdala, is fairly active, while the part of the brain that works with the amygdala to balance its passionate nature, becomes less active. This will reveal impulses and toxic blocks that may be hidden from consciousness.

Maybe God is warning you about something in your dreams. I once dreamed that two crazed men with huge daggers were attacking me, my husband and our four children on a beach. Well, three weeks after having this dream, this actually happened. In the dream God showed me how to pray out of the situation to survive. When the attack happened, I remembered the dream, and thank goodness I obeyed the instructions. We all survived; not one of us was harmed, even though we were being slashed at. It was as though God had called down heavenly hosts to protect us, and they did.

I have learned through this dream and many others to listen and act when God speaks to me through dreams. Maybe you are not forgiving someone, so your prayers are not being answered. It could be God has spoken to you on numerous occasions about this, but you haven't listened. Now He graciously nudges you in your dreams.

The crucial first step to using your dreams as part of the detox process is simply deciding to remember them (that is part of your free will), and the benefits will follow.

Brain Sweep

GATHER
- As you think about your dreams, especially when you first wake up, notice what your five senses are telling you. Are there any toxic memories or thoughts that even fleetingly cross your mind?

REFLECT
- *Reflect* on how you felt in your dream. Ask yourself, "How does what I can remember make me feel?"
- What do you think your dream means? What is God trying to tell you? What are some things you might need to change in your life? What fears might you need to conquer?

JOURNAL

- Now write down your dreams onto paper. As you *journal* or Metacog™, do you notice any patterns? Do you notice words or images that repeatedly come to mind? They can be early warning signs that something is wrong with your body or something of this nature.
- *Journaling* your dreams is the first step in dream analysis, a complex undertaking worthy of a book of its own. You don't have to be a specialist to understand how dreams relate to your body as well as mind.
- Simply writing down the story and feelings of your dream is shown to increase your blood and chemical flow, helping the detox process. Write down everything, even the fragmented bits, and always ask yourself how you feel.
- As you write, you draw valuable information into the conscious mind and out of the memory networks of your mind.

REVISIT

- Journaling about your dreams works over time. You may write things down but find its days or weeks before you understand the meaning; keep looking back for those hidden pearls of wisdom. As you *revisit* what you have written, are there any patterns?

REACH

- What are you learning from your dreams? Let God reveal what He wants you to do with the information.

15
CHAPTER
TOXIC SEEDS

This member of the Dirty Dozen, Toxic Seeds, grows roots that can strangle love and joy in our lives.

Do you have toxic seeds of unforgiveness in your life?

Forgiveness is a choice, an act of your free will. It enables you to release all those toxic thoughts of anger, resentment, bitterness, shame, grief, regret, guilt and hate. These emotions hold your mind in a nasty, vice-like grip. As long as these unhealthy toxic thoughts dominate your mind, you will not be able to grow healthy new thoughts and memories.

Forgiveness starts with repentance, which unmasks older pathways in the nerve circuits of the brain and then, as you forgive, reorganizes them by rebuilding new memories over the old. Besides the unmistakable importance of forgiveness in Scripture, now there is increasing scientific evidence that forgiveness gives us healthier and happier lives (there are more than a hundred studies showing the healing power of forgiveness).[9]

When we don't forgive, thoughts of the painful act will cause fear in the amygdala (the library for emotions), which causes stress chemicals, raises levels of stress hormones and increases blood pressure and heart rate. When people hold onto their anger and past trauma, the stress response stays active, making them sick mentally and physically.

Researchers using functional magnetic resonance imaging found that different parts of the brain are activated positively when people think about choosing to forgive rather than getting revenge. As we choose to forgive, the amygdala-frontal cortex link (see Part Three) becomes very active, calming the amygdala, and the stress response and toxic memory that caused the unforgiveness in the first place are changed.[10]

It is often said that forgiveness leads to the ability to love. You cannot love if you have not really forgiven and released those who have wronged you. Scientific research proves that love is good for your health.

You can't change the past, but God's Word and science show that changing how you think about past hurt can reduce its impact on you and the resulting likelihood of stress-related illness. We change how we think through repentance and forgiveness.

The world of psychological counseling is finally realizing a lot of mental health problems people experience are caused by unforgiveness. In fact, 94% of mental health counselors feel it is appropriate to bring up the issue of forgiveness.[11]

Of course Jesus has been telling us to forgive for over 2,000 years.

When we forgive, we are not making excuses for someone's behavior; we are letting go of the person and letting God sort them out. It is a choice that demonstrates great courage.

Let's jump right in!

 **Brain Sweep**

GATHER
- As you think about forgiveness, or maybe the lack of forgiveness in your life, notice what your five senses are telling you. Are there any toxic memories or thoughts that even fleetingly cross your mind?
- Who has hurt you?
- Who has harmed you?
- Who has made you feel unworthy?
- Who has said something about you that shocked you?
- What has happened to you in the past that still creates feelings of pain, bitterness and resentment when you remember it?

REFLECT
- Repentance precedes forgiveness. We are not supposed to hang onto any of the negative emotions that arise out of pain in some form or another, because God tells us that we are to cast all our cares on Him (see 1 Peter 5:7). As you *reflect* on your answers also ask yourself, "What am I holding onto?"

JOURNAL
- Now pour out your thoughts onto paper. As you *journal* or Metacog™, do you notice any patterns? Do you notice words or images that repeatedly come to mind?

REVISIT
- When you see something written down about the incidents, how you feel, and the consequences of unforgiveness, it becomes easier to make the right choice – to forgive.

- We get serious when we write down the names of people we need to forgive. As you *revisit* what you have written, make a list of those you need to forgive – this list might even include yourself.

REACH
- Now it's time to *reach* beyond the toxic thoughts and bring health and life to your mind. It's time for God's Word to come alive in your life, so make a decision to forgive. What steps can you take to move beyond the pain of the past and into your future? What steps can you take to see healthy relationships restored? What steps can you take to bring restoration into your environment?
- The benefits are worth it: God forgives you; your stress levels decrease; your blood pressure is lowered; relationships improve; and pain and chronic illness are reduced.
- You can choose!

16
CHAPTER
TOXIC FAITH

Toxic Faith is a wiley member of the Dirty Dozen. He slinks in when you least expect him.

There is no doubt, you are a spiritual being. No healing of toxic waste in your mind and body will be complete unless you address Toxic Faith.

A growing body of scientific research confirms that prayer and actively developing your spiritual life increases frontal lobe activity, thickness, intelligence and overall health.[12]

Have you had a negative experience in the church? Have people of faith hurt you?

When you sweep away those experiences, you will be able to see God and His unfailing love for you, past any negative memories that may be polluting your spiritual life.

Jesus wants us to be completely healed – spirit, soul and body.

Without a doubt, my Christianity is the guiding belief of my life. It gives me hope in a world that is often without hope and an anchor in truth and reality. God is my Intelligent Designer, and this level of information flows from the Holy Spirit.

These Brain Sweep questions will truly help you move past any seeds of Toxic Faith!

 **Brain Sweep**

GATHER

- As you think about your walk of faith, notice what your five senses are telling you. Are there any toxic memories or thoughts that come to mind?
- Are you reading the Bible daily?
- Are you praying all the time?
- Are you spending time with God building a relationship?
- Are you going to church?
- Are you part of a church community?
- Are you feeding your spirit?

REFLECT

- As you read a passage of Scripture that might particularly speak to your heart, stop after one or two verses and ask yourself what you have read.
- Answer yourself. Discuss it with yourself.

JOURNAL

- Write down what you are learning in a journal or Metacog™ to consolidate your memory.
- Write any memory verse that comes to mind onto the Metacog™ or in your *journal.*
- Be organized and have purpose to your Bible study.
- As you *journal* or Metacog™, do you notice any patterns? Do you notice words or images repeatedly coming to mind?

REVISIT

- Go through your journal or Metacog™ so you can reinforce what you are learning.
- Do you have anything to add?
- How can you apply the information to your life?

- Personalize what you have learned; take ownership of the information.

REACH

- How can you *reach* beyond the seeds of Toxic Faith? Practice using the principles learned; for example, if you need healing, speak life and healing scriptures over yourself.
- Make the Word of God come alive in your life.
- Find what you are passionate about and apply the Word to it, because through your passion and gifting you can become closer to God.

17
CHAPTER
TOXIC LOVE

Love is one of God's greatest gifts, but if Toxic Seeds are planted, a love betrayed can also be one of the most hurtful experiences in our lives.

When you experience emotions such as appreciation, love, care and compassion, studies show clear changes in the patterns of activity in the autonomic nervous system, immune system, hormonal system, brain and heart. Such physiological changes may help explain the observed connection among positive emotions, improved health and increased longevity.

In contrast, some of the brain systems activated in people who are lovesick show activation in an area of the brain associated with risk-taking. When you don't give or experience love, there is a physical reaction in your brain expressed as stress in your body.[13]

Science shows and the Bible tells us that when people operate in love they do extraordinary things. In fact, we are wired for love; it is as fundamental as hunger or thirst. Love activates what is called the pleasure-reward system in the brain, and the neurotransmitter dopamine (a brain chemical that gives you a high and makes your thinking sharp and clear) is released, which helps with focus, attention and healthy thought growth. In fact the dopamine-rich regions of the brain are so strong that when our thinking becomes toxic, they are hijacked, turning the good into bad and love into addictions.[14]

Interestingly, though many consider the heart as only the source of love, research shows that the heart considers and "thinks" about information received from the brain. This implies the heart has opinions of its own. It acts as a still, small voice checking our thoughts for accuracy, integrity and wisdom. The "mini-brain" of the heart literally functions like a conscience.[15]

The voice of your heart is a gentle nudge, or a sense of warning. Always listen.

Your heart is not just a pump. It is your body's strongest biological oscillator, which means it has the ability to pull every other system of the body into its own rhythm. When the heart is at peace and filled with love, the entire body under the direction of the brain, feels peace and love as well.

The opposite is also true. When your thought life is filled with toxic emotions, your heart is heavy and burdens your body and mind. In effect, your heart amplifies what is going on in the brain.

When you experience the love of God and of people, your heart speeds up its communication with the mind and body through your blood vessels. Life is in the blood, the body's transport system, and the heart is in charge of making sure the transport works. Health travels from the brain to the heart in electrical signals and from there to the rest of the body.

New brain research shows that love deactivates the brain regions associated with negative emotions, social judgment and judgment of other people's intentions and emotions, giving you a strong sense of longing.

Love helps us feel others' pain and empathize with them, especially those close to us. We are wired to love and have concern for each other.

Remember the biblical teaching that love is patient and kind, not jealous, proud, boastful or rude; it is not selfish, does not keep a track of wrongs, is quick to believe the best, wants justice and never fails (see 1 Corinthians 13).

 **Brain Sweep**

GATHER
- Are you listening to the quiet guiding voice of your heart?
- Are you feeling peaceful or disturbed?
- What is the message from your heart?

REFLECT
- Are you *reflecting* on all the blessings in your life?
- Do you have an attitude of gratitude?
- Are you *reflecting* on painful thoughts?
- Do you focus on and spend time with people who bring you joy and happiness?
- Do you focus on happy memories of good times or anticipate special happy events?
- Do you allow fear to cloud messages from your heart?

JOURNAL
- Now pour out your thoughts onto paper. As you *journal* or Metacog™, do you notice any patterns? Do you notice words or images that repeatedly come to mind?
- Write down all the good things God has done for you. Write down all the wonderful things about your spouse, your children, your parents, your best friends and yourself.

REVISIT
- Are you giving and receiving love?
- Check your stress levels.

REACH
- Make a commitment to walk in love; that is, make an intentional choice to love others no matter what.
- Meditate on the definition of love found in 1 Corinthians 13.
- That kind of commitment requires practice, practice and more practice, but the benefits are beyond belief. How can you start making that a commitment in your life?
- Maybe you are having a disagreement with someone. To detox from this, put yourself in that person's shoes, make an effort to see the issue(s) from their perspective. Try this for 24 hours. Then, focus on doing what Jesus would do – give 100% to that person without expecting anything back. You will be pleasantly surprised at what happens.

18
CHAPTER
TOXIC TOUCH

Human connection is one of the most important elements of living in community with one another. However, sometimes Toxic Touch, a member of the Dirty Dozen, turns what is supposed to be a healing and healthy human connection into an ugly area of toxic thinking.

We know how hurtful abuse is. When touch is harmful it is never, ever acceptable. We also know that forgiveness is imperative to move beyond past hurt that still may be fresh in our minds.

But sometimes we don't realize that another aspect of Toxic Touch is actually the lack of touch.

In fact, lack of touch (called "cutaneous deprivation") causes emotional problems, affects our intellect and physical growth, and weakens the immune system. Research even shows touch-deprivation causes negative change in the brain (neuroplasticity), laying the patterns for aggression and violence.

Our need for touch creates a "skin-hunger."

Touch is literally described as "one of the most essential elements of human development," a "critical component of the health and growth of infants" and a "powerful healing force." It is the healing force that cured baby rhesus monkeys of stress symptoms, trauma and depression, according to 1950's and 1960's studies completed by the late

Wisconsin University psychologist Harry Harlow. The importance of touch is only a recent scientific discovery, but 2000 years ago, Jesus touched those He healed when He walked the earth; He held and loved and comforted through touch.

In Harlow's research, a fake mother made of wire and cloth with milk bottles instead of breasts raised baby monkeys. The babies were fed but not touched, hugged, or held. Before long, they all showed signs of stress and depression. The signs vanished after researchers brought in an older monkey who hugged and cuddled them. What happened to these baby monkeys? Touch broke the negative reaction chains that feelings of emotional deprivation had caused in their brains.[16]

It isn't difficult to see that brain-damaged adults are creating brain-damaged children at an ever-increasing rate.

Back in the 40's the seed for this research was sown when a compassionate doctor – Rene Spitz – started an anguished quest to discover why babies were dying even when their nutrition, medicine and surroundings were good. What he discovered was that these babies were dying from touch-deprivation. The brain will rewire negatively in several important areas when our skin, a large organ, rich in nerves, doesn't get affectionate touch and therefore isn't able to send those signals to our brain.[17]

There is a hunger inside of us more powerful than our hunger for food; we are wired by a loving God for loving touch. Today, grade schools and high schools are filled with severely withdrawn and troublesome, unruly children and teens who have given up hope of affectionate pleasure and happiness, all because they have been deprived of touch. There is overwhelming evidence that the United States is one of the most violent and one of the least physically affectionate societies on this planet. In the U.S. it is estimated only 25% of children come from a functional home in which adequate attachment occurs.[18]

Listen to this story of a little 4-year-old boy who was placed in boarding school: the first night when he was crying for his mother he was locked in a dark cupboard by his caretakers. He was deprived of touch from his mother and father and the teachers at the boarding school, who were, more likely than not, deprived of loving touch by their mothers.

Despite this trauma, the boy grew to be very successful in business, but he always carried the burdens of life, often depressed, sad and oversensitive. He married a very loving woman, which changed him, and had four children of his own. Despite his loving wife, he still struggled with bouncing his children on his knees because he had never had that experience. But Jesus touched him through his wife and his four children and his thirteen grandchildren. Although he never became a "touchy-feely" dad and granddad, he was able to pour out love through his actions. When you looked into his eyes, you were smothered in his love. This man was my dad.

So that gentle pat on the hand, or the kind tap on the back or the welcoming hug you gave someone may very well have unblocked a toxic cycle in their brain. We are instrumental in helping heal each other through something as simple as loving touch. That touch can shift a person's day from a disaster to a success.

Those around you will benefit from touch as well. Neuroscientists have discovered a very interesting function that neurons play when it comes to human interaction, such as empathy (identifying with and sharing in someone else's pain or joy). We have these amazing groups of neurons in the top and side of our brains (premotor cortex and inferior parietal cortex) that get all excited and start firing in the same part of the brain that initiates a hug. Neuron firing also happens in the person who made the decision to hug someone as they identified with their issue and reached out in love.

We are designed for relationship – man is not meant to be alone, so it would make sense to have a brain wired to make touch happen. This is also why we love to hear other people's stories; the neurons help make them real for us as we learn from each other.[19]

We each have our own inner and natural pharmacy that produces all the drugs we ever need to run our body-mind in precisely the way it was designed to run.

Of course, prescription drugs have their place. They do save lives. However, they are only a means to an end and usually have serious side effects. Human touch, on the other hand, releases the body's natural chemicals in a healing process that optimizes your feelings of well-being. Many animal and human studies show the benefits of touch in alleviating depression and other illnesses that have physical symptoms. Missing, exaggerated, muted or otherwise distorted perceptions and responses become toxic thoughts. Affectionate touch is an essential "nutrient" to overcoming these toxic thoughts and to retaining normal brain functioning.

Touch is one of the physical things you can do to change your mental processes.

Quite simply, the human being thrives on touch. To give and receive loving touch is good for your mind-body health, not to mention the great health impact touch has on others.

 **Brain Sweep**

GATHER
- Ask yourself, "What amount of touch have I received today? Is it great or distorted or maybe even missing?"
- Did you hug your husband or wife today and tell them you love them?
- Did you lavish affection on your children? Or did you push them aside into high chairs, playpens, car seats, baby beds, nurseries, the back yard or put them in front of the TV?

REFLECT
- Become consciously aware of how the touch you received today, or the lack of it, made you feel.
- Talk to your children, spouse and parents about how good you feel when you get an encouraging hug.
- Ask them how they felt when they were or weren't hugged.

JOURNAL
- Now write out and illustrate your thoughts on paper. As you *journal* or Metacog™, do you notice any patterns? Do you notice words or images that repeatedly come to mind?
- Do you need a "Monkey-Hug Action Plan" to increase your intelligence and health and help detox your thought life? If so, *journal* this.
- Are you causing negative toxic wiring in yourself and in those you love by the distance you keep? If you are not sure, make a mental note each time you affectionately touch someone.

REVISIT
- As you *revisit* what you have written, do you see any patterns?

- Don't invade a person's space – always start by extending your hand and making eye contact. This is a request for consent to gently give a hug or some other form of touch if the other person is comfortable with it.

REACH

- What effect has affectionate touch had on the people around you?
- Did it make a difference in their life?
- Did it make a difference in your life?
- Studies show that following a month of treatment, massage recipients showed lower cortisol, again suggesting reduced stress and increased dopamine levels. Go for a massage!
- Great "monkey-hugs" include hugs, handshakes, pats on the shoulder, or a comforting rub on the back.

19
CHAPTER
TOXIC SERIOUSNESS

This member of the Dirty Dozen hates to have fun, and hates it when you have fun.

Having fun is more infectious than a virus; in fact, it is viral. Try not to laugh when those around you are in convulsions of hysterical laughter. Try to keep having a bad day when you have just had a good belly laugh.

Having fun will detox your thought life, improve your health and make you clever to boot. It's one of the most powerful antidotes to stress you will ever find, and it's free. Fun is a tremendous resource God built into your brain to bring perspective into your life, help surmount problems, add sizzle to your relationships, and make you feel good.

Many studies show why laughter deserves to be known as "the best medicine." It releases an instant flood of feel-good chemicals that boost the immune system and almost instantly reduce levels of stress hormones. For example, a really good belly laugh can make cortisol drop by 39% and adrenalin by 70%, while the "feel-good hormone," endorphin, increases by 29%. It can even make growth hormones skyrocket by 87%! Other research shows how laughter boosts your immune system by increasing immunity levels and disease-fighting cells.[20]

Just look at some of the myriad of benefits of having fun. Humor gets both sides of your brain working together, which is one of the keys to releasing potential. Some studies even suggest that laughter helps to increase flexibility of thought and is as effective as aerobic exercise in boosting body-mind health.

According to research, laughing 100 to 200 times a day is equal to 10 minutes of rowing or jogging! Laughter quite literally dissolves distressing toxic emotions because you can't feel mad or sad when you laugh: endorphins are released, making you feel so great and at peace that toxic thoughts can't get out of your brain fast enough.

Fun protects your heart, because when you laugh and enjoy yourself, your body releases chemicals that improve the function of blood vessels and increase blood flow, protecting against heart attack. Fun reduces damaging stress chemicals quickly, which, if they hang around in your body for too long, will make you mentally and physically sick. Fun and laughter also increase your energy levels.[21]

Wow . . . can you afford not to laugh?

Are you stressed? Well, find something to laugh about. Laughing is a wonderful form of stress-reduction. When we play, we are stretching our emotionally expressive ranges and preparing for detox.

Having fun through play and laughter is the cheapest, easiest and most effective way to control toxic thoughts and emotions and their toxic stress reaction. It rejuvenates the mind, body and spirit and gets positive emotions flowing. Smile – this is the beginning of laughter. When you hear laughter, gravitate toward it and let it wash all over you. The brain science of laughter is that it expands – the more you get, the more you want and, believe me, the more you need.

Our emotions are what connect us and give us a sense of unity, a feeling that we are part of something greater. Quite simply, developing a playful point of view will enable us to live longer, happier and healthier lives. God and now science are both telling us this.

Brain Sweep

GATHER
- As you think about the importance of laughter, or maybe the lack of fun in your life, notice what your five senses are telling you. Are there any toxic memories or thoughts that even fleetingly cross your mind?
- You have 5 senses – get into the habit of *gathering* fun, not pain, through them.

REFLECT
- Humor shifts perspective. As you *reflect*, observe how your own attitude changes as you allow fun into your life.

JOURNAL
- Now pour out your thoughts onto paper. As you *journal* or Metacog™, do you notice any patterns? Do you notice words or images that repeatedly come to mind?
- How often do you have fun or do something that you really enjoy?
- Have you ever just thought fun thoughts? Observe yourself over 21 days – you're either filled with fun or you are just plain boring.
- *Journal* a fun plan for your life.
- Plan to have fun as much as you plan to work out at the gym.

REVISIT

- Is your fun level increasing?
- Are you having fun regularly?
- Do you feel healthier and cleverer yet? If not, you are not having enough fun.

REACH

- Have you ever made a list of all your blessings? Doing so will override and weaken the negative thoughts and start to break them down in your brain. Negative thoughts become a barrier to fun.
- When did you last play a board game, card game or anything with your family or friends?
- When did you last talk nonsense and laugh so hysterically with someone so that tears ran down your cheeks?
- How often do you remember funny incidents of the past and relive them and laugh about them?
- Do you ever tell, make or read jokes?
- Have you ever tried laughing away defensiveness?
- Have you ever spent time with fun, playful people? They are contagious with a virus you want to catch.
- Do you laugh at yourself?
- Have you ever tried to develop a playful point of view? You will love it!
- Do you watch funny movies?
- When did you last play with a pet?
- Do you take yourself too seriously?
- When did you last share your embarrassing moments and laugh?
- Do you ever look for the humor in a bad situation?
- Do you ever watch your children have fun and learn how to have fun with them?

20
CHAPTER
TOXIC HEALTH

No one hates exercise and a healthy lifestyle more than this member of the Dirty Dozen, Toxic Health. He knows that when health invades your body, your mind and your spirit are next.

The value of exercise in this context has less to do with building muscles or burning calories than with getting the heart to pump faster and more efficiently. Increased blood flow nourishes and cleanses the brain and organs, supplying the brain with much-needed oxygen, making you feel mentally sharper. If you break into a sweat, you will also get the added benefit of mood improvement, prompted by the release of endorphins.

Exercise helps generate new brain cells and stimulates the production and release of BDNF (neuronal growth factor), which plays a really important role in changing thinking.[22]

There are many different types of aerobic exercise, from running to cycling. Even better are forms of exercise, such as brisk walking, that allow you time to stop and smell the roses, which helps calm and focus your mind. Central to this detox step is finding a form of exercise you enjoy, so you are far more likely to keep it up and enjoy its detoxing benefits.

 **Brain Sweep**

GATHER
- As you think about health, or maybe the lack of health and balance in your life, notice what your five senses are telling you. Are there any toxic memories or thoughts that even fleetingly cross your mind?
- What exercise are you doing regularly?
- Is it enough?

REFLECT
- Are you not exercising because you don't know what to do? Get some advice.
- If you are already exercising and serious about sports, get advice to make sure you are managing the process effectively.
- Are you sure exercise isn't becoming your god? Because it is addictive.

JOURNAL
- Write down your goals so you are organized.
- Do you want to lose weight?
- Do you want to increase proficiency?
- Do you want to work toward competitions?

REVISIT
- Check up on your written goals weekly.
- Get someone to help monitor you if necessary.

REACH
- Do it!
- How can you take action?

21
CHAPTER
TOXIC SCHEDULES

Rush, rush, rush! Hurry, hurry, hurry! Busy, busy, busy! This is the voice of the last member of the Dirty Dozen, Toxic Schedules.

The ever-increasing pace of life, called the "acceleration syndrome," is causing a global epidemic of "hurry sickness." Two symptoms are the dizzying speed at which we live and the excessive amount of living we force into our lives.

Many "solutions" offered, such as time management and learning to delegate and prioritize, are having the opposite effect. They actually increase the pace of life by creating a time squeeze and encouraging us to cram even more into an hour. These things only aggravate the problem they were supposed to address.

They make you time poor, and that poverty extends to your thought life. Your time is precious and belongs only to you. Every day you make choices about how you are going to spend your time. Learning to spend it wisely is an important part of controlling your thoughts.

The next time you think you don't have time for exercise or relaxation, think again. The reality is simply that you have chosen to fill your time with activities and things other than exercise and relaxation. Focus on what is good for you. Like many of us, you probably manage to fill your day with an endless list of things, small and large, which are not vital to your health. If you constantly focus on the little things, you might ignore the big things that ultimately determine your health, success and happiness.

The next time you think you don't have time for exercise or relaxation, think again. The reality is simply that you have chosen to fill your time with activities and things other than exercise and relaxation.

Every organ and muscle in your body has a sympathetic (stressed) state and a parasympathetic (relaxed) state. Both of these systems are part of the autonomic nervous system. Researchers at the Institute of HeartMath (an organization that researches the effects of positive emotions on physiology, quality of life and performance) have found that "busy-rush syndrome" creates toxic emotions, disrupts the autonomic nervous system, leads to erratic heart rhythms and a myriad of other health problems.[23]

If you take the time to do things that generate healthy thoughts and their positive emotions – love, respect and kindness – the result will be more coherent heart rhythms. This rhythm is a balance between the sympathetic (accelerates the heartbeat) and the parasympathetic (slows down the heartbeat) nervous systems. Therefore, relaxing is not just a luxury; it's a necessity. You need to balance the sympathetic and parasympathetic systems. Toxic thoughts throw off this balance and predispose you to sickness.

If you don't build relaxation into your lifestyle you will become a less effective thinker, defeating your ability to accomplish the mental tasks that stole your relaxation in the first place. In fact, for the brain to function like it should, it needs regroup/consolidation time. If it doesn't get this, it will send out signals in the form of high-level stress hormones, some of which are epinephrine, norepinephrine and cortisol. If these chemicals constantly flow, they create a "white noise" effect that increases anxiety and blocks clear thinking and the processing of information.

Simply put, relaxation is never a waste of time.

We need 10 to 20 minutes of some sort of down time every one-and-a-half to two hours. If we do not allow ourselves this recovery time, we will simply wear ourselves out.[24]

The scary thing is, the losses may not be that evident initially, but after 3-4 hours your clear thinking and processing will drop off to all-time lows. The whole electrical-chemical building of networks is affected by increasing stress levels in the brain, making us feel agitated, frustrated, tearful and even aggressive.

What should you do in those 10-20 minutes?

Work on your thoughts with imagination and fun-filled mental exercises. You can think about a great scripture and imagine applying it to your life. You could imagine that next holiday or that pair of shoes or golf clubs you think would look great on your feet or in your hand respectively. Imagine anything relaxing. Remember: when you imagine, it actually happens in your brain, so when you imagine fun things, all kinds of good chemicals flow, preparing you for the next round of concentration.

Brain Sweep

GATHER
- Is your life one of constant scrambling and extreme workloads?

- At the end of the day, do you feel frustrated that you haven't achieved enough?
- Do you tend to focus on what you haven't done rather than what you have done?
- Do you know when to stop working and take a break?
- Are you or your children overshadowed by a fear of not living up to someone's expectations? If yes, then your relaxation (peace) will be stolen because this toxic thought will drive you all the time.
- Have you simply lost your ability to switch off and take a break?

REFLECT
- Have you ever thought about the benefits of relaxation?
- Have you ever thought about the negative effects on your mind and health if you don't relax?

JOURNAL
- Have you ever taken the time to write down all the things you love to do?
- Have you ever worked out a relaxation plan for 1 week, 1 month or 1 year?
- Work into your day a 10-20 minute downtime every couple of hours.

REVISIT
- Ask yourself how can you follow through?

REACH
- Learn to balance your work and rest before it's too late. Make a list of what you would eliminate from your life if you only had six months to live. I suggest you also list what you would really like to do in those six months to make you as happy and content as possible. You will be amazed at how much waste you will cut out of your daily schedule and what important things you have been keeping out of it!

- What do you notice?
- Imagine (visualize), for example, a relaxing scene like walking along a beach. Remember: when you think of an activity in your mind, it has the same physical effect in your brain as if you were actually doing the activity.
- Meditation – focused awareness, interactive and engaged healthy thinking resulting in understanding. This is what you do when you read the Word of God and when you learn something new.
- Pray. What scriptures come to mind?
- Daily quiet time all to yourself, relaxing, doing little or nothing.
- Get a massage (it's part of touch therapy).
- Sleep – the ultimate relaxer! You need between seven to nine hours of sleep a night and more on the weekends. If you are one of the many chronically sleep deprived, you need to address that. Quality and quantity of restful sleep are prerequisites for controlling toxic thoughts, emotions and body weight. When you sleep the brain sorts out your thinking for the next day and consolidates memories.
- Exercise – brisk walking, cycling, swimming and stretching.

CONCLUSION

It is important to recognize that your journey to freedom from the Dirty Dozen has just begun. You *will* move forward with confidence.

When you make the commitment to stand and fight the Dirty Dozen, you will discover you have made a decision that will impact the rest of your life. You can make that decision and live in freedom!

What scientists and researchers, with their new tools and techniques of evaluation and analysis, have discovered recently may leave you stunned. This book was created alongside the scientific arena to stun you, excite you and motivate you to recognize the truth: God has given you the gift of free will. This gift empowers you to take control of the very thing that creates everything about who you are – your thought life.

May you take this gift and use it for the great things it was designed for. Be part of changing the world.

ACKNOWLEDGEMENTS

Writing a book is one of those things you never do alone – the teams of people involved in the project enrich the whole experience. I have a passion for the brain and the science of thought, one which God birthed in me, and I am so privileged to be able to fulfill my passion in this way: writing books and helping people see that they can choose to change and improve their lives.

There are so many special people to thank from the bottom of my heart, people who have helped me achieve this dream: My amazing husband and children, to whom I have dedicated this book . . . thank you.

My family who always believe in whatever I do: Mom, Christiane, Joanne, Peter and Elizabeth, and Dad who is up there with the cloud of witnesses.

Anne and Peter Pretorius, you believed in my message and opened your hearts to me, encouraging me from the conception to the birth of the first edition of this book . . . thank you.

Jimmy and Terry, you truly operate "in Proverbs." You have opened my eyes to my vision, and you have opened doors that are astounding. May the blessings pour back into your lives and business . . . thank you.

James and Betty Robison, your passion and excitement to help others is an anointing that touched my heart. Thank you for the privilege of being on your show and for, quite literally, bringing this book into the world to help set people free.

Carolyn, you are simply amazing. You streamline my thinking, you challenge my brain and you are such fun. Each project with you is a delight . . . thank you.

The whole Inprov team, who are exceptional and display the spirit of excellence by going above and beyond the call of duty . . . thank you.

Joyce Meyer, you have inspired me for years with your incredible understanding of the human mind. Thank you for the privilege of being on your show and for believing in me.

Marilyn Hickey . . . I have always admired and loved your deep understanding of the Word of God, which you make simple to apply. Thank you for the privilege of being on your show.

To my special friends who have each played a significant role in my life and this book: Sterna; Jimmy and Kirie; Peter and Mercy; Sue and Andrew; Leon and Shirley.

APPENDIX A

A Metacog™ is a way of seeing your thoughts on paper, and evaluating the way you think and what you think about. It helps detox your thought life by allowing you to follow your thought patterns. Journaling in this way helps you gain full understanding of the situation you are reflecting over.

It's really simple; you group patterns that radiate from a central point. Each pattern linked to the central point creates a branch. Don't limit yourself to just writing in straight lines. Then continue to develop each of the branches by linking more detailed patterns. As you focus on the information, if there are word associations or groupings that seem to naturally flow together, group those on a page. Draw a picture or diagram to go along with that thought expression. Add color or texture. The process can continue until you have explored every nuance of your thought.

AN EXAMPLE OF A METACOG™

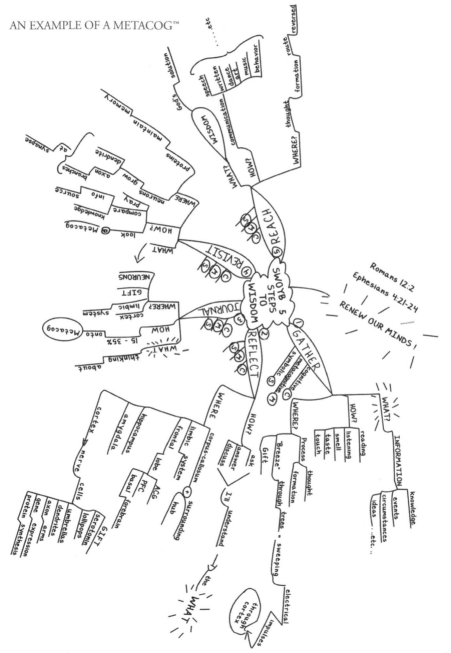

END NOTES

PART 1
1.

- Doidge, N. 2007. The Brain that Changes Itself: Stories of personal triumph from the frontiers of brain science. Penguin Books. USA.
- Kandel, E.R. 2006. In Search of Memory: The emergence of a new science of mind. W.W. Norton & Company. NY.
- Lipton, B. 2008. The Biology of Belief: Unleashing the power of consciousness, matter and miracles. Mountain of Love Productions. USA.

2.

- Colbert, D. 2003. Deadly Emotions: Understand the mind-body-spirit connection that can heal or destroy you. Thomas Nelson. Nashville, Tennessee.
- Diamond, M. & Hopson, J. 1999. Magic Trees of the Mind: How to nurture your child's intelligence, creativity and healthy emotions from birth through adolescence. Penguin. USA.
- Kandel, In Search of Memory.
- Martin, K. 2009. www.biolchem.ucla.edu/labs/martinlab/links.htm.
- Pert, C.B. 1997. Molecules of Emotion: Why You Feel the Way You Feel. Simon and Schuster. UK.

3.

- Colbert, Deadly Emotions.
- Pert, Molecules of Emotion.

4.

- Doidge, The Brain that Changes Itself.
- "Ghost in Your Genes." http://www.pbs.org/wgbh/nova/genes/.
- Harvard Health Publications. 2009. https://www.health.harvard.edu/newsweek/ Prevalence-and-treatment-of-mental-illness-today.htm.
- Kopp, M.S. & Rethelyi, J. 2004. "Where Psychology Meets Physiology: Chronic stress and premature mortality – the Central-Eastern European health paradox." Brain Research Bulletin. 62: 351-367.
- Lipton, The Biology of Belief.
- Martin, www.biolchem.ucla.edu/labs/martinlab/links.htm.
- McEwan, B.S. & Lasley, E.N. 2002. The End of Stress as We Know It. National Academies Press. Washington.
- McEwan, B.S. and Seeman, T. 1999. "Protective and Damaging Effects of Mediators of Stress: Elaborating and testing the concepts of allostasis and allostatic load." Annals of the New York Academy of Sciences. 896: 30-47.
- National Institute of Mental Health. 2009. www.nimh.nih.gov/health/topics/ statistics/index.shtml.
- Segerstrom, S.C. and Miller, G.E. 2004. "Psychological Stress and the Human Immune System: A meta-analytic study of 30 years of inquiry." Psychological Bulletin. Vol. 130, N04. 601-630.

5.

- Freeman, W.J. 1995. Societies of Brains: A study in the neuroscience of love and hate. Hillsdale, NJ.
- Leaf, C.M. 1990. "Mind Mapping: A therapeutic technique for closed head injury." Masters Dissertation, University of Pretoria.
- Lipton, The Biology of Belief.
- Pert, Molecules of Emotion.

6.
- Kandel, In Search of Memory.
- Restak, R. 2009. Think Smart: A neuroscientists prescription for improving your brain performance. Riverhead Books. New York.

7.
- Doidge, The Brain that Changes Itself.
- Lipton, The Biology of Belief.
- Peters, T. 2003. Playing God? Genetic Determinism and Human Freedom, 2nd Ed. Routledge. NY.

8.
- Leaf, "Mind Mapping: A therapeutic technique for closed head injury."
- Leaf, C.M. 1997. "The Mind Mapping Approach: A model and framework for Geodesic Learning." Unpublished D. Phil Dissertation, University of Pretoria.

9.
- Kandel, In Search of Memory.
- Restak, Think Smart.

10.
- Bach-y-Rita, P. & Collins, C.C. et al 1969. "Vision Substitution by Tactile Image Projection in Nature." 221 (5184): 963-64.
- Kandel, In Search of Memory.

11.
- Doidge, The Brain that Changes Itself.
- Lipton, The Biology of Belief.
- Ramachandran, V.S. & Blakeslee, S. 1998. Phantoms in the Brain. William Morrow. NY.
- Taub, E., Uswatte, G. et al. 2005. "Use of CI Therapy for Plegic Hands after Chronic Stroke." Presentation at the Society for neuroscience. Washington DC.

12.
- Leaf, "Mind Mapping: A therapeutic technique for closed head injury."
- Leaf, "The Mind Mapping Approach: A model and framework for Geodesic Learning."

PART 2
1.
- Dispenza, J. 2007. "Evolve Your Brain: The science of changing your brain." Health Communications, Inc. FL.
- Harvard. https://www.health.harvard.edu/topic/stress.
- Harvard Health Publications. https://www.health.harvard.edu/newsweek/Prevalence-and-treatment-of-mental-illness-today.htm
- Kandel, E.R., Schwartz, J.H. & Jessell, T.M. eds. 1995. Essentials of Neural Science and Behavior. Appleton & Lange. USA.
- Perlemutter, D. & Coleman, C. 2004. The Better Brain Book. Penguin Group. USA.
- Pert, Molecules of Emotion.

2.
- Kopp & Rethelyi, "Where Psychology Meets Physiology."
- Lipton, The Biology of Belief.
- McEwan and Seeman, "Protective and Damaging Effects of Mediators of Stress."

3.   Lipton, The Biology of Belief.
4.
- Colbert, Deadly Emotions.

- Harvard. https://www.health.harvard.edu/topic/stress.
- Lipton, The Biology of Belief.
- Pert, Molecules of Emotion.

5.
- Dispenza, "Evolve Your Brain."
- Doidge, The Brain that Changes Itself.
- Freeman, Societies of Brains.
- Pert, Molecules of Emotion.

6. Lipton, The Biology of Belief.

7.
- Dispenza, "Evolve Your Brain."
- Kopp & Rethelyi, "Where Psychology Meets Physiology."
- Pert, Molecules of Emotion.

8.
- Colbert, Deadly Emotions.
- Gazzaniga, M.S. 2004. Ed. The New Cognitive Neurosciences. Bradford Books. The MIT Press.
- Pert, Molecules of Emotion.

9.
- Colbert, Deadly Emotions.
- Dispenza, "Evolve Your Brain."
- Pert, Molecules of Emotion.
- Restak, Think Smart.

10.
- Colbert, Deadly Emotions.
- Dispenza, "Evolve Your Brain."
- Kagan, A. & Saling, M.M. 1988. An Introduction to Luria's Aphasiology Theory and Application. Witwatersrand University Press. Johannesburg, SA.
- Pert, Molecules of Emotion.
- Restak, Think Smart.

11.
- Doidge, The Brain that Changes Itself.
- Kalivas, P.W. & Volkow N.D. 2005. "The Neural Basis of Addiction: A pathology of motivation and choice." Am J Psychiatry. 162: 1403-1413.
- Kandel, In Search of Memory.
- Kosslyn, S.M. & Koenig, O. 1995. Wet Wind: The new cognitive neuroscience. Free. NY.
- Pert, Molecules of Emotion.

12. Colbert, Deadly Emotions.

13.
- Childre, D. & Martin, H. 1999. The Heartmath Solution. Harper-Collins. San Francisco, CA.
- Heart Science. www.heartmath.org/research/science-of-the-heart.html.

14.
- Childre & Martin, The Heartmath Solution.
- Heart Science. www.heartmath.org/research/science-of-the-heart.html.

15.
- Childre & Martin, The Heartmath Solution.
- Heart Science. www.heartmath.org/research/science-of-the-heart.html.

16.
- Colbert, Deadly Emotions.
- Doidge, The Brain that Changes Itself.
- Harvard. https://www.health.harvard.edu/topic/stress.
- Hawkins, D.B. 2001. When Life Makes You Nervous: New and effective treatments for anxiety. Cook Communication. USA.
- Jacobs, B.L., Van Praag, H. et al. 2000. "Depression and the Birth and Death of Brain Cells." American Scientist, 88 (4):340-46.

- Matheny, K.B. & McCarthy, J. 2000. Prescription for Stress. Harbinger Publications. USA.
- Pert, Molecules of Emotion.
- Restak, Think Smart.

17.
- McEwan & Lasley, The End of Stress as We Know It.
- "Mind/Body Connection: How emotions affect your health." http://familydoctor. org/online/famdocen/home/healthy/mental/782.html.
- Perlemutter & Coleman, The Better Brain Book.
- Pert, Molecules of Emotion.
- Pert, C. et al. 1973. "Opiate Agonists and Antagonists Discriminated by Receptor Binding in the Brain." Science. (182): 1359-61.

18.
- McEwan & Lasley, The End of Stress as We Know It.
- "Mind/Body Connection." http://familydoctor.org/online/famdocen/home/ healthy/mental/782.html.
- Perlemutter & Coleman, The Better Brain Book.
- Pert, Molecules of Emotion.
- Pert, "Opiate Agonists and Antagonists Discriminated by Receptor Binding in the Brain."
- Sarno, J. 1998. The Mind-Body Prescription. Werner Books. NY.

19.
- Pert, Molecules of Emotion.
- Taubes, G. 2008. Good Calories, Bad Calories: Fats, carbs and the controversial science of diet and health. Anchor Books. NY.

20.
- Colbert, Deadly Emotions.
- Pert, Molecules of Emotion.
- Taubes, Good Calories, Bad Calories.

PART 3
1.
- Diamond & Hopson, "Magic Trees of the Mind."
- Restak, R. 2000. "Mysteries of the Mind." National Geographic Society.
- Restak, Think Smart.

2. Nader, K., Schafe, G.E. et al. 2000. "Fear Memories Require Protein Synthesis in the Amygdala for Reconsolidation after Retrieval." Nature. 406(6797): 722-26.

3.
- Pert, Molecules of Emotion.
- Restak, "Mysteries of the Mind."

4. Leaf, C.M. 2008. Switch on Your Brain 5 Step Learning Process. Switch on Your Brain USA. Dallas, TX.

5.
- Leaf, C.M. 1997. "An Altered Perception of Learning: Geodesic Learning." Therapy Africa. 1 (2), October 1997, p. 7.
- Leaf, C.M. 1998. "An Altered Perception of Learning: Geodesic Learning: Part 2." Therapy Africa. 2 (1), January/February 1998, p. 4.
- Leaf, C.M. 1992. "Evaluation and Remediation of High School Children's Problems Using the Mind Mapping Therapeutic Approach." Remedial Teaching. Unisa, 7/8, September 1992.
- Leaf, "Mind Mapping: A therapeutic technique for closed head injury."
- Leaf, C.M. 1985. "Mind Mapping as a Therapeutic Intervention Technique." Unpublished workshop manual.
- Leaf, C.M. 1989. "Mind Mapping as a Therapeutic Technique." Communiphon. South African Speech-Language-Hearing Association. 296, pp. 11-15.
- Leaf, Switch on Your Brain 5 Step Learning Process.
- Leaf, C.M. 2005. Switch on Your Brain: Understand your unique intelligence profile and maximize your potential. Tafelberg. Cape Town, SA.

- Leaf. C.M. 2002. Switch on Your Brain with the Metacognitive-Mapping Approach. Truth Publishing.
- Leaf, C.M. 1990. "Teaching Children to Make the Most of Their Minds: Mind Mapping." Journal for Technical and Vocational Education in South Africa. 121, pp. 11-13.
- Leaf, C.M. 1997. "The Development of a Model for Geodesic Learning: The Geodesic Information Processing Model." The South African Journal of Communication Disorders, Vol. 44, pp. 53-70.
- Leaf, "The Mind Mapping Approach: A model and framework for Geodesic Learning."
- Leaf, C.M. 1993. "The Mind Mapping Approach (MMA): Open the door to your brain power; learn how to learn." Transvaal Association of Educators Journal (TAT).
- Leaf, C.M. 1997. "The Move from Institution Based Rehabilitation (IBR) to Community Based Rehabilitation (CBR): A paradigm shift." Therapy Africa. 1 (1) August 1997, p. 4.
- Leaf, C.M. 2007. Who Switched Off My Brain? Controlling toxic thoughts and emotions. Switch on Your Brain USA. Dallas, TX.
- Leaf, C.M. 2007. "Who Switched Off My Brain? Controlling toxic thoughts and emotions." DVD series. Switch on Your Brain. Johannesburg, SA.
- Leaf, C.M., Copeland M. & Maccaro, J. 2007. "Your Body His Temple: God's plan for achieving emotional wholeness." DVD series. Life Outreach International. Dallas, TX.
- Leaf, C.M., Uys, I.C. and Louw, B. 1998. "An Alternative Non-Traditional Approach to Learning: The Metacognitive-Mapping Approach." The South African Journal of Communication Disorders. 45, pp. 87-102.
- Leaf, C.M., Uys, I. and Louw. B., 1997. "The Development of a Model for Geodesic Learning: the Geodesic Information Processing Model." The South African Journal of Communication Disorders. 44.
- Leaf, C.M., Uys, I.C. and Louw, B. 1992. "The Mind Mapping Approach (MMA): A culture and language-free technique." The South African Journal of Communication Disorders. Vol. 40, pp. 35-43.

6.
- Dispenza, "Evolve Your Brain."
- Lipton, The Biology of Belief.
- Peters, Playing God?.
- Restak, Think Smart.

7.
- Iran-Nejad, A. & Chissom, B. 1988. "Active and Dynamic Sources of Self-regulation." Paper presented at the Annual Meeting of the American Psychological Association. Atlanta, GA.
- Leaf, "The Mind Mapping Approach: A model and framework for Geodesic Learning."

8. Harrell, K.D. 1995. Attitude is Everything: A tune-up to enhance your life. Kendall/Hunt Publishing Company. USA.

9.
- Kandel, E.R., Schwartz, J.H. & Jessell, T.M. eds. 2000. Principles of Neural Science, 4th Ed. McGraw-Hill. NY.
- Kosslyn & Koenig, Wet Mind.
- Springer, S.P. and Deutsch, G. 1998. Left Brain, Right Brain. W.H. Freeman & Company. NY.

10.
- Colbert, Deadly Emotions.
- Wright, N.H. 2005. Finding Freedom from Your Fears. Fleming H. Revell. Grand Rapids.

11.
- Kandel, In Search of Memory.

* Nader & Schafe, "Fear Memories Require Protein Synthesis in the Amygdala for Reconsolidation after Retrieval."

12.
* LeDoux, J. 2002. Synaptic Self: How our brains become who we are. NY.
* Pert, Molecules of Emotion.
* Restak, "Mysteries of the Mind."

13.
* LeDoux, Synaptic Self.
* Pert, Molecules of Emotion.

14.
* Freeman, Societies of Brains.
* Harvard University Gazette. 1998. "Sleep, dreams and learning." http://www.news. harvard.edu/gazette/1996/02.08/ResearchLinksSl.htm.l
* O'keefe, J. and Nadel, L. 1978. The Hippocampus as a Cognitive Map. Oxford University Press. NY.

15.
* Jacobs & Van Praag, "Depression and the Birth and Death of Brain Cells."
* Sapolsky, R.M. 1996. "Why Stress is Bad for Your Brain." Science. 273(5276): 749-50.
* Vythilingam, M. & Heim, C. "Childhood Trauma Associated with Smaller Hippocampal Volume in Women with Major Depression." American Journal of Psychiatry. 159(12): 2072-80.

16.
* Amua-Quarshie, P. Basalo-Cortical Interactions: The role of the basal forebrain in attention and alzheimer's disease. Unpublished Master's thesis. Rutgers University.
* Kosslyn & Koenig, Wet Mind.
* Nader & Schafe, "Fear Memories Require Protein Synthesis in the Amygdala for Reconsolidation after Retrieval."

17.
* Kandel, In Search of Memory.
* Kandel, Schwartz & Jessell, Principles of Neural Science.
* Martin, www.biolchem.ucla.edu/labs/martinlab/links.htm.
* Nader & Schafe, "Fear Memories Require Protein Synthesis in the Amygdala for Reconsolidation after Retrieval."

18.
* Decety, J., & Grezes, J. 2006. "The Power of Simulation: Imagining one's own and other's behavior." Brain Research. 1079, 4-14.
* Decety, J., & Jackson, P.L. 2006. "A Social Neuroscience Perspective of Empathy." Current Directions in Psychological Science. 15, 54-58.
* Pascuale-Leone, A. & Hamilton, R. 2001. "The Metamodal Organization of the Brain." in Casanova, C. & Ptito, eds., Progress in Brain Research Volume 134. Elsevier Science. San Diego, CA.

19.
* Decety & Grezes, "The Power of Simulation: Imagining one's own and other's behavior."
* Decety & Jackson, "A Social Neuroscience Perspective of Empathy."
* Pascuale-Leone & Hamilton, "The Metamodal Organization of the Brain."

20. Childre & Martin, The Heartmath Solution.

21.
* Leaf, Switch on Your Brain 5 Step Learning Process.
* Leaf, "The Mind Mapping Approach: A model and framework for Geodesic Learning."

22.
* Kandel, In Search of Memory.
* Kandel, Schwartz & Jessell, Principles of Neural Science.
* Martin, www.biolchem.ucla.edu/labs/martinlab/links.htm.
* Pascuale-Leone & Hamilton, "The Metamodal Organization of the Brain."

23.
* Amen, D. G. 1998. Change Your Brain Change Your Life. Three Rivers Press. NY.

- Diamond, M. 1988. Enriching Heredity: The impact of the environment on the brain. Free Press. NY.
- Kandel, Schwartz & Jessell, Essentials of Neural Science and Behavior.

24.
- Leaf, Switch on Your Brain 5 Step Learning Process.
- Leaf, Switch on Your Brain: Understand your unique intelligence profile and maximize your potential.

25. Leaf, "The Mind Mapping Approach: A model and framework for Geodesic Learning."

26.
- Merzenich, M.M. 2001. "Cortical Plasticity Contributing to Childhood Development." in McClelland, J.L. & Siegler, R.S. (Eds.). Mechanisms of Cognitive Development: Behavioural and neural perspectives. Lawrence Erlbaum Associates. Mahwah, NJ.
- Nader & Schafe, "Fear Memories Require Protein Synthesis in the Amygdala for Reconsolidation after Retrieval."
- Pascuale-Leone & Hamilton, "The Metamodal Organization of the Brain."

27.
- Kandel, In Search of Memory.
- Lipton, The Biology of Belief.

PART 4

1.
- Kandel, In Search of Memory.
- Nader & Schafe, "Fear Memories Require Protein Synthesis in the Amygdala for Reconsolidation after Retrieval."

2.
- Diamond, & Hopson, "Magic Trees of the Mind."
- Fodor, J. 1983. The Modularity of Mind. MIT/Bradford. Cambridge.
- Kandel, In Search of Memory.

3. Pert, "Opiate Agonists and Antagonists Discriminated by Receptor Binding in the Brain."

4. Pulvermuller, F. 2002. The Neuroscience of Language. Cambridge University Press.

5.
- Epigenetics. 2004. http://www.sciencemag.org/feature/plus/sfg/resources/res_epi genetics.dtl.
- Epigenetics. 2006. http://discovermagazine.com/2006/nov/cover.
- Epigenetics. 2006. http://www.ehponline.org/members/2006/114-3/focus.html.
- Lipton, The Biology of Belief.
- Lipton, B.H., Bensch, K.G., et al. 1991. "Microvessel Endothelial Cell Transdifferentiation: Phenotypic Characterization." Differentiation. 46: 117-133.
- Peters, Playing God?.

6. Kandel, In Search of Memory.

7.
- Solms, M. 1999. http://www.abc.net.au/rn/talks/8.30/helthrpt/stories/s44369. htm.
- Stickgold, R., Hobson, R. et al. 2001. "Sleep, Learning, and Dreams: Offline memory reprocessing." Science. 294 (554): 1052-57.

8.
- Pert, "Opiate Agonists and Antagonists Discriminated by Receptor Binding in the Brain."
- Solms, M. 2000. "Forebrain Mechanisms of Dreaming are Activated from a Variety of Sources." Behavioral and Brain Sciences. 23(6): 1035-1040; 1083-1121.

9.
- Forgiveness. 2005. http://www.aolhealth.com/conditions/five-for-2005-five-reasons-to-forgive.
- Forgiveness. 2004. https://www.health.harvard.edu/press_releases/power_of_ forgiveness.

10.
- Clark, A.J. 2005. "Forgiveness: a Neurological Model." Medical Hypotheses. 65):649-54.
- Forgiveness. http://www.aolhealth.com/conditions/five-for-2005-five-reasons-to-forgive.
- Forgiveness. https://www.health.harvard.edu/press_releases/power_of_forgiveness.
11. Forgiveness. http://www.aolhealth.com/conditions/five-for-2005-five-reasons-to-forgive.
12.
- Beauregard, M. & O'Leary, D. 2007. The Spiritual Brain. Harper Collins. NY.
- Religion and Science. 2009. http://www.time.com/time/health/arti cle/0,8599,1879016,00.html.
- Religion and Science. 2008. http://www.liebertonline.com/doi/abs/10.1089/acm.2007.0675.
13. Freeman, Societies of Brains.
14.
- Dispenza, "Evolve Your Brain."
- Doidge, The Brain that Changes Itself.
- Kandel, In Search of Memory.
- Love and Neuroscience. 2009. http://www.nature.com/nature/journal/v457/n7226/full/457148a.html.
- Merzenich, "Cortical Plasticity Contributing to Childhood Development."
15. Childre & Martin, The Heartmath Solution.
16. Harlow, H.1998. http://www.pbs.org/wgbh/aso/databank/entries/bhharl.html.
17.
- Doidge, The Brain that Changes Itself.
- Spitz, R. 1983. http://www.pep-web.org/document.php?id=PPSY.002.0181A.
18.
- Hatfied, R. 1994. http://faculty.plts.edu/gpence/PS2010/html/Touch%20and%20 Human%20Sexuality.htm.
- Hatfield, W. Robert, W. 1994. "Touch and Human Sexuality." in Bullough, V. & Bullough, B. & Stein, A. (Eds.). Human Sexuality: An Encyclopedia. Garland Publishing. NY.
19. Rizzolotti, G. 2008. http://www.scholarpedia.org/article/Mirror_neurons.
20.
- Colbert, Deadly Emotions.
- Cousins, N. 1981. Anatomy of an Illness as Perceived by the Patient. Bantam. NY.
- Fountain, D. 2000. "God, Medicine, and Miracles." The Spiritual Factors in Healing. Random House.
21.
- Cousins, Anatomy of an Illness as Perceived by the Patient.
- Laughter. 2007. http://thehealingpoweroflaughter.blogspot.com/2007/07/how-marx-brothers-brought-norman.html.
- Laughter. 2006. http://heyugly.org/LaughterOneSheet2.php.
22. Vaynman S., & Gomez-Pinilla. 2005. "License to Run: Exercise impacts functional plasticity in the intact and injured central nervous system by using neurotrophins." Neurorehabilitation and Neural Repair. 19(4): 283-95.
23. Heart Science. http://www.heartmath.org/research/science-of-the-heart.html.
24.
- Leaf, Switch on Your Brain 5 Step Learning Process.
- Relaxation. 2005. http://www.scientificamerican.com/article.cfm?id=want-clear-thinking-relax.
- Restak, Think Smart.

RECOMMENDED READING

The concepts I teach in this book cover a very wide spectrum and years of reading, researching and working with clients, in private practice and schools and business corporations. If I had to provide all the citations to document the origin of each fact for complete scientific scholarship that I have used, there would be almost as many citations as words. So I have used a little flexibility to write this book in a more popular style, helping me to communicate my message as effectively as I can. There are only a few citations in the actual text that are more general, and the book list that follows is less of a bibliography (which would be too long) and more of a recommended reading list of some of the great books and scientific articles I have used in my research.

1. Adams, H.B. & Wallace, B. 1991. "A Model for Curriculum Development: TASC." Gifted Education International. 7, pp. 194-213.
2. Alavi, A., Hirsch, L.J. 1991. "Studies of Central Nervous System Disorders with Single Photon Emission Computed Tomography and Positron Emission Tomography: Evolution over the past 2 decades." Semin. Nucl. Med. 21 (1), Jan.: 51-58.
3. Alesandrini, K.L. 1982. "Imagery – Eliciting Strategies and Meaningful Learning." Journal of Educational Psychology. 62, pp. 526-530.
4. Allen, D. & Amua-Quarshie, P. et.al. 2004. Mental Health at Work (White Paper) by Pecan Ltd, Peckham. http://www.pecan.org.uk/Group/Group.aspx?id=41212R. London, UK.
5. Allport, D.A. 1980. "Patterns and Actions: Cognitive mechanisms and content specific." in Claxton, G.L. (Ed.) Cognitive Psychology: New Directions. Routledge & Kegan Paul. London.
6. Amen, D.G. 2008. Magnificent Mind at Any Age. Harmony Books. USA.
7. Amen, D.G. 1998. Change Your Brain Change Your Life. Three Rivers Press. NY.
8. Amend, A.E. 1989. "Defining and Demystifying Baroque, Classic and Romantic Music." Journal of the Society for Accelerative Learning and Teaching. 14 (2), pp. 91-112.
9. Amua-Quarshie, P. 2009. Basalo-Cortical Interactions: The role of the basal forebrain in attention and alzheimer's disease. Unpublished Master's thesis. Rutgers University. Newark, NJ.
10. Amua-Quarshie, P. 2008. http://news.rutgers.edu/focus/isue.2008-03-26.6300207636/article.2008-03-26.8293146433.
11. Anderson, J.R. 1985. Cognitive Psychology and Its Complications, 2nd Ed. W.H. Freeman. NY.
12. Arnheim, R. 1979. "Visual Thinking in Education." in Sheikll, A. and Shaffer, J. (Eds.) The Potential of Fantasy and Imagination. pp. 215-225. Brandon House. NY.
13. Atkins, R.C. 1990. Dr. Atkins Health Revolution. Houghton Mifflin Company. Boston, MA.
14. Atkins, R.C. 2003. Dr. Atkins New Diet Revolution. Ebury Press. London.
15. Atkins, R.C. 2003. New Diet Cook Book. Ebury Press. London.
16. Bach-y-Rita, P. & Collins, C.C. et al 1969. "Vision Substitution by Tactile Image Projection in Nature." 221(5184): 963-64.
17. Bancroft, W.J. "Accelerated Learning Techniques for the Foreign Language Classroom." Per Linguam. 1 (2), pp. 20-24.
18. Barker, J.A. 1987. Discovering the Future: A question of paradigms. Charterhouse Productions, S.A. Breweries. SA.

19. Bartlett, F.C. 1932. Remembering: A study in experimental and social psychology. Cambridge University Press. Cambridge.
20. Baxter, R., Cohen, S.B. & Ylvisaker, M. 1985. "Comprehensive Cognitive Assessment." in Ylvisaker, M. Head Injury Rehabilitation: Children and adolescents. pp. 247-275. College-Hill Press. CA.
21. Beauregard, M. & O'Leary, D. 2007. The Spiritual Brain. Harper Collins. NY.
22. Bereiter, L. 1985. "Toward a Solution of the Learning Paradox." Review of Educational Research. 55, pp. 201-225.
23. Berninger, V., Chen, A. & Abbot, R. 1988. "A Test of the Multiple Connections Model of Reading Acquisition." International Journal of Neuroscience. 42, pp. 283-295.
24. Bishop, J.H. 1989. "Why the Apathy in American High Schools?" Educational Researcher. 18 (1), pp. 6-10.
25. Block, N. & Dworkin, G. 1976. The I.Q. Controversy. Pantheon. NY.
26. Bloom, B.S. 1984. "The Z Sigma Problem: The search for methods of group instruction as effective as one-to-one tutoring." Educational Researcher. 13 (6), pp. 4-16.
27. Bloom, F.E. Beal, M.F et al. eds. 2003. The Dana Guide to Brain Health. Dana Press. NY.
28. Bloom, L. & Lahey, M. 1978. Language Development and Language Disorders. Wiley & Sons. Canada.
29. Boller, K. & Rovee-Collier, C. 1992. "Contextual Coding and Recording of Infant's Memories." Journal of Experimental Child Psychology. 53 (1), pp. 1-23.
30. Borkowski, J.G., Schneider, W. & Pressley, M. 1989. "The Challenges of Teaching Good Information Processing to the Learning Disabled Student." International Journal of Disability, Development and Education. 3 (3), pp. 169-185.
31. Botha, L. 1985. "SALT in Practice: A report on progress." Journal of the Society for Accelerative Learning and Teaching. 10 (3), pp. 197-199.
32. Botkin, J.W., Elmandjra, M. & Malitza, M. 1979. No Limits to Learning. Bridging the Human Gap: A report of the club of rome. Pergammon Press. Oxford and NY.
33. Boyle, P. 2009. http://esciencenews.com/articles/2009/06/15/having.a.higher. purpose.life.reduces.risk.death.among.older.adults.
34. Bransford, J.D. 1979. Human Cognition. Wadsworth. Belmont, CA.
35. Brain and Mind Symposium. Columbia University. 2004. http://c250.columbia. edu/c250_events/symposia/brain_mind/brain_mind_vid_archive.html.
36. Braten, I. 1991. "Vygotsky as Precursor to Metacognitive Theory, II: Vygotsky as metacognitivist." Scandinavian Journal of Educational Research. 35 (4), pp. 305-320.
37. Briggs, M.H. 1993. "Team Talk: Communication skills for early intervention teams." Journal of Childhood Communication Disorders. 15 (1), pp. 33-40.
38. Broadbent, D.E. 1958. Perception and Communication. Pergammon Press. London.
39. Brown, A.L. 1978. "Knowing When, Where and How to Remember: A problem of meta-cognition." in Glaser, R. (Ed.) Advances in Instructional Psychology. Erlbourne. Hillsdale, NJ.
40. Bunker, V.J., McBurnett, W.M. & Fenimore, D.L. 1987. "Integrating Language Intervention throughout the School Community." Journal of Childhood Communication Disorders. 11 (1), pp. 185-192.
41. Buzan, T. 1991. Use Both Sides of Your Brain. Plume. NY.
42. Buzan, T. 2000. Head First. Thorsons. London.

43. Buzan, T. & Dixon, T. 1976. The Evolving Brain. Wheaten & Co, Ltd. Exetar.
44. Buzan, T. & Keene, R. 1996. The Age Heresy. Ebury Press. London.
45. Bynum, J. 2002. Matters of the Heart. Charisma House. USA.
46. Byron, R. 1986. Behavior in Organizations: Understanding and managing the human side of work, 2nd Ed. Allyn & Bacon. Boston, MA.
47. Byron, R. & Byrne, D. 1984. Social Psychology: Understanding human interaction, 4th Ed. Allyn & Bacon. Boston, MA.
48. Calvin, W. & Ojemann, G. 1994. Conversations with Neil's Brain. Addison-Wesley. Reading, MA.
49. Campbell, B., Campbell, L. and Dickinson, D. 1992. Teaching and Learning through Multiple Intelligences. New Horizons for Learning. Seattle, WA.
50. Campione, J.C., Brown, A.L. & Bryant, N.R. 1985. "Individual Differences in Learning and Memory." in Sternberg, R.J. (Ed.) Human Abilities: An information processing approach. pp. 103-126. West Freeman. NY.
51. Capra, F. 1982. "The Turning Point: A new vision of reality." The Futurist. 16 (6), pp. 19-24.
52. Caskey, O. 1986. "Accelerating Concept Formation." Journal of the Society for Accelerative Learning and Teaching. 11 (3), pp. 137-145.
53. Chi, M. 1985. "Interactive Roles of Knowledge and Strategies in the Development of Organized Sorting and Recall." in Chipman, S.F., Segal, J.W. & Glaser, R. (Eds.) Thinking and Learning Skills Vol 2. Lawrence Erlbaum & Assoc. Hillsdale, NJ.
54. Childre, D. & Martin, H. 1999. The Heartmath Solution. Harper-Collins. San Francisco, CA.
55. Clancey, W. 1990. "Why Today's Computers Don't Learn the Way People Do." Paper presented at the Annual Meeting of the American Educational Research Association. Boston, MA.
56. Clark, A.J. 2005. "Forgiveness: A neurological model." Medical Hypotheses. 65):649-54.
57. Cloete, P. 2003. Lecture Series. Tel: (044) 884 0863.
58. Colbert, D. 2001. The Bible Cure for Memory Loss. Siloam Press. FL.
59. Colbert, D. 2003. Deadly Emotions: Understand the mind-body-spirit connection that can heal or destroy you. Thomas Nelson. Nashville, TN.
60. Concise Oxford Dictionary, 9th Ed. 1995. Oxford University Press. Oxford.
61. Cook, N.D. 1984. "Colossal Inhibition: The key to the Brain Code." Behavioral Science. 29, pp. 98-110.
62. Costa, A. L. 1984. "Mediating the Metacognitive." Educational Leadership. 42 (3), pp. 57-62.
63. Cousins, N. 1981. Anatomy of an Illness as Perceived by the Patient. Bantam, NY.
64. Cousins, W. 1979. "Anatomy of an Illness as Perceived by the Patient." New England Journal of Medicine. 295(1976) 1458-63.
65. Crick, F.H.C. 1981. "Thinking about the Brain." Scientific American. 241 (3), p. 228.
66. Crick, F. The Astonishing Hypothesis: The scientific search for the soul. Charles Scribner & Sons. NY.
67. Damasio, A. R. 1999. The Feeling of What Happens: Body and motion in the making of consciousness. Harcourt, Brace & Company. NY.
68. Damico, J.S. 1987. "Addressing Language Concerns in the Schools: The SLP as consultant." Journal of Childhood Communication Disorders. 11 (1), pp. 17-40.
69. Dartigues, J-F. 1994. "Use It or Lose It." Omni. Feb. 1994, p. 34.
70. De Andrade, L.M. 1986. "Intelligence's Secret: The limbic system and how to mobilize it through suggestopedy." Journal of the Society for Accelerative Learning and Teaching. 11 (2), pp. 103-113.
71. De Capdevielle, B. 1986. "An Overview of Project Intelligence." Per Linguam. 2 (2), pp. 31-38.
72. Decety, J., & Grezes, J. 2006. "The Power of Simulation: Imagining one's own and other's behavior." Brain Research. 1079, 4-14.

73. Decety, J., & Jackson, P.L. 2006. "A Social Neuroscience Perspective of Empathy." Current Directions in Psychological Science. 15, 54-58.
74. Decety, J. & Grezes, J. 1996. "Neural Mechanisms Subserving the Perception of Human Actions." in http://www.scribd.com/doc/16500831/Neural-Mechanisms-Sub-Serving-the-Perception-of-Human-Actions-Decety-Grezes-1999.
75. Derry, S.J. 1990. "Remediating Academic Difficulties through Strategy Training: The acquisition of useful knowledge." Remedial and Special Education. 11 (6), pp. 19-31.
76. Dhority, L. 1991. The ACT Approach: The artful use of suggestion for integrative learning. PLS Verlag GmbH, Bremen, West Germany.
77. Diamond, S. & Beaumont, J. (Eds.) Hemisphere Function of the Human Brain. pp. 264-278.
78. Diamond, M. 1988. Enriching Heredity: The impact of the environment on the brain. Free Press. NY.
79. Diamond, M. & Hopson, J. 1999. "How to Nurture Your Child's Intelligence, Creativity and Healthy Emotions from Birth through Adolescence." Magic Trees of the Mind. Penguin. USA.
80. Dienstbier, R. 1989. "Periodic Adrenalin Arousal Boosts Health Coping." Brain-Mind Bulletin. 14(9a).
81. Dispenza, J. 2007. "Evolve Your Brain: The science of changing your brain." Health Communications, Inc. FL.
82. Dobson, J. 1997. How to Build Confidence in Your Child. Hodder & Stoughton. Great Britain.
83. Doidge, N. 2007. The Brain that Changes Itself: Stories of personal triumph from the frontiers of brain science. Penguin Books. USA.
84. Edelman, G.M. & Mountcastle, V.B. (Eds.). The Mindful Brain. MIT Press. Cambridge, MA.
85. Edelman, G.M. & Tononi, G. 2000. A Universe of Consciousness: How matter becomes imagination. Basic Books. NY.
86. Edwards, B. 1979. Drawing on the Right Side of the Brain. J.P. Torcher. Los Angeles, CA.
87. Einstein, A. 1979. The Human Side: New glimpses from his archives. Princeton University Press. Princeton, NJ.
88. Einstein, A. 1999. "Albert Einstein: Person of the century." Time. Dec 31, 1999.
89. Enchanted Loom. 1986. BBC Productions.
90. Entwistle, N. 1988. "Motivational Factors in Students' Approaches in Learning." in Schmeck, R.R. (Ed.) Learning Strategies and Learning Styles. pp. 21-51. Plenum. NY.
91. Entwistle, N.J. & Ramsdon, P. 1983. Understanding Student Learning. Croom Helm. London.
92. Epigenetics. 2004. http://www.sciencemag.org/feature/plus/sfg/resources/res_epi genetics.dtl.
93. Epigenetics. 2006. http://discovermagazine.com/2006/nov/cover.
94. Epigenetics. 2006. http://www.ehponline.org/members/2006/114-3/focus.html.
95. Eriksen, C.W. & Botella, J. 1992. "Filtering Versus Parallel Processing in RSVP Tasks." Perception and Psychophysics. 51 (4), pp. 334-343.
96. Erskine, R. 1986. "A Suggestopedic Math Project Using Non Learning Disabled Students." Journal of the Society for Accelerative Learning and Teaching. 11 (4), pp. 225-247.
97. Farah, M.J., Peronnet, F. et al. 1990. "Brain Activity Underlying Visual Imagery: Event related potentials during mental image generation." Journal of Cognitive Neuroscience. 1:302-16.
98. Faure, C. 1972. Learning to Be: The world of education today and tomorrow. UNESCO. Paris.
99. Feldman, D. 1980. Beyond Universals in Cognitive Development. Ablex Publishers. Norwood, NJ.
100. Feuerstein, R. 1980. Instrumental Enrichment: An intervention program for cognitive modifiability. University Park Press. Baltimore, MD.

101. Feuerstein, R., Jensen, M., Roniel, S. & Shachor, N. 1986. "Learning Potential Assessment." Assessment of Exceptional Children. Haworth Press, Inc.
102. Flavell, J.H. 1978. "Metacognitive Development." in Scandura, J.M. & Brainerd, C.J. (Eds.) Structural/Process Theories of Complete Human Behaviour. Sijthoff & Noordoff. The Netherlands.
103. Flavell, P. 1963. The Developmental Psychology of Jean Piaget. Basic Books. NY.
104. Fodor, J. 1983. The Modularity of Mind. MIT/Bradford. Cambridge.
105. Fountain, D. 2000. God, Medicine, and Miracles: The spiritual factors in healing. Random House.
106. Forgiveness. 2004. https://www.health.harvard.edu/press_releases/power_of_forgiveness.
107. Forgiveness. 2005. http://www.aolhealth.com/conditions/five-for-2005-five-reasons-to-forgive.
108. Franzsen, S. 2003. Lecture series. Pretoria, SA.
109. Frassinelli, L., Superior, K. & Meyers, J. 1983. "A Consultation Model for Speech and Language Intervention." ASHA. 25 (4), pp. 25-30.
110. Freeman, W.J. 1995. Societies of Brains: A study in the neuroscience of love and hate. Lawrence Erlbaum Associates. Hillsdale, NJ.
111. Galton, F. 1907. Inquiries into Human Faculty and Its Development. L. M. Dent. London.
112. Gardner, H. 1981. The Quest for Mind: Piaget, Levi-Strauss, and the Structuralist Movement. University of Chicago Press. Chicago, IL and London.
113. Gardner, H. 1985. Frames of Mind. Basic Books. NY.
114. Gardner, H. & Wolfe, D.P. 1983. "Waves and Streams of Symbolization." in Rogers, D. & Slabada, J.A. (Eds.) The Acquisition of Symbolic Skills. Plenum Press. London.
115. Gazzaniga, M.S. 1977. Handbook of Neuropsychology. Plenum. NY.
116. Gazzaniga, M.S. 2004. (Ed.) The New Cognitive Neurosciences. Bradford Books. The MIT Press.
117. Gelb, M. 1988. Present Yourself. Jalmar Press. Los Angeles, CA.
118. Gerber, A.1987. "Collaboration between SLP's and Educators: A continuity education process." Journal of Childhood Communication Disorders. 11(1-2): 107-125.
119. "Ghost in Your Genes." http://www.pbs.org/wgbh/nova/genes/.
120. Glaser, R. 1977. Adaptive Education: Individual diversity and learning. Holt, Rhinehort and Winston. NY.
121. Glasser, M.D. 1986. Control Theory in the Classroom. Harper & Row. NY.
122. Goldberg, E. & Costa, L.D. 1981. "Hemisphere Differences in the Acquisition and Use of Descriptive Systems." Brain and Language. 14, pp. 144-173.
123. Gould, S. 1973. "Commission on Nontraditional Study." Diversity by Design. Jossey-Bass. San Francisco, CA.
124. Gould, S. 1981. The Mismeasure of Man. W.W. Norton. NY.
125. Griffiths, D.E. 1964. "Behavioural Science and Educational Administration." 63rd Yearbook of the National Society for the Study of Education. NSSE. Chicago, IL.
126. Gungor, E. 2007. There is More to the Secret. Thomas Nelson. Nashville, TN.
127. Guyton, A.C & Halle, J.E. Textbook of Medical Physiology, 9th Ed. W.D. Saunders. Philadelphia, PA.
128. Haber, R.N. 1981. "The Power of Visual Perceiving." Journal of Mental Imagery. 5, pp. 1-40.
129. Halpern, S. & Savary, L. 1985. Sound Health: The music and sounds that make us whole. Harper & Row. San Francisco, CA.
130. Hand, J.D. 1986. "The Brain and Accelerative Learning." Per Linguam. 2 (2), pp. 2-14.
131. Hand, J.D. & Stein, B.L. 1986. "The Brain and Accelerative Learning, Part II: The brain and its functions." Journal of the Society for Accelerative Learning and Teaching. 11(3), pp. 149-163.
132. Harlow, H. 1998. http://www.pbs.org/wgbh/aso/databank/entries/bhharl.html.

133. Harrison, C.J. 1993. "Metacognition and Motivation." Reading Improvement. 28 (1), pp. 35-39.
134. Harrell, K.D. 1995. Attitude is Everything: A tune-up to enhance your life. Kendall/Hunt Publishing Company. USA.
135. Hart, L. 1983. Human Brain and Human Learning. Longman. NY.
136. Harvard. https://www.health.harvard.edu/topic/stress.
137. Harvard Health Publications. 2009. https://www.health.harvard.edu/newsweek/ Prevalence-and-treatment-of-mental-illness-today.htm.
138. Harvard University Gazette. 1998. "Sleep, Dreams and Learning." http://www. news.harvard.edu/gazette/1996/02.08/ResearchLinksSl.html.
139. Harvard University Gazette. 1996. "Aging Brains Lose Less Than Thought." http:/ www.hno.harvard.edu/gazette/1996/10.03/AgingBrainsLose.html.
140. Harvard University Gazette. 2003. "Childhood Abuse Hurts the Brain." http:/www. hno.harvard.edu/gazette/2003/05.22/01-brain.html.
141. Harvard Health Publications. 2009. "Positive Psychology: Harnessing the power of happiness, personal strength and mindfulness." https://www.health.harvard.edu/ special_health_reports/Positive-Psychology.
142. Hatfield, W. & Robert W. 1994. "Touch and Human Sexuality." in Bullough, V. & Bullough, B. & Stein, A. (Eds.). Human Sexuality: An Encyclopedia. Garland Publishing. NY.
143. Hatfied, R. 1994. http://faculty.plts.edu/gpence/PS2010/html/Touch%20and%20 Human%20Sexuality.htm.
144. Hatton, G.I. 1997. "Function-related Plasticity in the Hypothalamus." Annual Review of Neuroscience. 20:375-97.
145. Hawkins, D.B. 2001. When Life Makes You Nervous: New and effective treatments for anxiety. Cook Communication. USA.
146. Hayman, J.L. 1975. "Systems Theory and Human Organization." in Zalatimo, Sulerman, D. & Sterman, P.J. (Eds.). A Systems Approach to Learning Environments. MEDED Projects, Inc. Roselle, NJ.
147. Heart Science. http://www.heartmath.org/research/science-of-the-heart.html.
148. Healy, J. "Why Kids Can't Think: Bottom Line." Personal. 13 (8), pp. 1-3.
149. Hinton, G.E. & Anderson, J.A. 1981. Parallel Models of Associate Memory. Erlsbaum. Hillsdale, NJ.
150. Hochberg, L.R., Serruya, G.M. et al. 2006. "Neuronal Ensemble Control of Prosthetic Devices by a Human with Tetraplegia." Nature. 442(7099): 164-71.
151. Holden, C. 1996. "Child Development: Small refugees suffer the effects of early neglect." Science. 305:1076-1077.
152. Holford, P. 1997. The Optimum Nutrition Bible. Piatkus. London.
153. Holford, P. 1999. The 30-Day Fat Burner Diet. Piatkus. London.
154. Holford, P. 2003. Optimum Nutrition for the Mind. Piatkus. London.
155. Holt, J. 1964. How Children Fail. Pitman. NY.
156. Hubel, D.H. 1979. "The Brain." Scientific American. 24 (13), pp. 45-53.
157. Hunter, C. & Hunter F. 2008. Laugh Yourself Healthy. Christain Life. FL.
158. Hyden, H. 1977. "The Differentiation of Brain Cell Protein, Learning and Memory." Biosystems. 8(4), pp. 22-30.
159. Hyman, S.E. 2005. "Addiction: A disease of learning and memory." Am J Psychiatry. 162:1414-22.
160. Iaccino, J. 1993. Left Brain-Right Brain Differences: Inquiries, evidence and new approaches. Lawrence Erlbaum & Associates. Hillsdale, NJ.
161. Iran-Nejad, A. 1987. "The Schema: A long-term memory structure of a transient functional pattern." in Teireny, R.J., Anders, P. & Mitchell, J.N. (Eds.) Understanding Reader is Understanding. pp. 109-128. Lawrence Erlbaum & Associates. Hillsdale, NJ.
162. Iran-Nejad, A. 1989. "Associative & Nonassociative Schema Theories of Learning." Bulletin of the Psychonomic Society. 27 pp. 1-4.

163. Iran-Nejad, A. & Chissom, B. 1988. "Active and Dynamic Sources of Self-Regulation." Paper presented at the Annual Meeting of the American Psychological Association. Atlanta, GA.

164. Iran-Nejad, A. & Ortony, A. 1984. "A Biofunctional Model of Distributed Mental Content, Mental Structures, Awareness and Attention." The Journal of Mind and Behaviour. 5, pp. 171-210.

165. Iran-Nejad, A., Ortony, A. & Rittenhouse, R.K. 1989. "The Comprehension of Metaphonical Uses of English by Deaf Children." American Speech-Language-Association. 24, pp. 551-556.

166. Iran-Nejad, A. 1990. "Active and Dynamic Self-Regulation of Learning Processes." Review of Educational Research. 60 (4), pp. 573-602.

167. Jacobs, B., Schall, M. & Scheibel, A.B. 1993. "A Quantitative Dendritic Analysis of Wernickes Area in Humans: Gender, hemispheric and environmental factors." Journal of Comparative Neurology. 327(1): 97-111.

168. Jacobs, B.L. Van Praag, H. et al. 2000. "Depression and the Birth and Death of Brain Cells." American Scientist. 88 (4):340-46.

169. Jensen, A. 1980. Bias in Mental Testing. Free Press. NY.

170. Jensen, E. 1995. Brain-Based Learning and Teaching. Process Graphix. South Africa.

171. Johnson, D.W., Johnson, R.T. & Holubec, E. 1986. Circles of Learning: Co-operation in the Classroom. Interaction Book Company. Edina, MN.

172. Johnson, J.M. 1987. "A Case History of Professional Evolution from SLP to Communication Instructor." Journal of Childhood Communication Disorders. 11 (4), pp. 225-234.

173. Jorgensen, C.C. & Kintsch, W. 1973. "The Role of Imagery in the Evaluation of Sentences." Cognitive Psychology. 4, pp. 110-116.

174. Kagan, A. & Saling, M. 1988. An Introduction to Luria's Aphasiology Theory and Application. Witwatersrand University Press. Johannesburg, SA.

175. Kalivas, P.W. & Volkow N.D. 2005. "The Neural Basis of Addiction: A pathology of motivation and choice." Am J Psychiatry. 162: 1403-1413.

176. Kandel, E.R. 2006. In Search of Memory: The emergence of a new science of mind. W.W. Norton & Company. NY.

177. Kandel, E.R, Schwartz, J.H. & Jessell, T.M. (Eds.) 2000. Principles of Neural Science, 4th Ed. McGraw-Hill. NY.

178. Kandel, E.R, Schwartz, J.H. & Jessell, T.M. (Eds.) 1995. Essentials of Neural Science and Behavior. Appleton & Lange. USA.

179. Kandel. 2000. http://nobelprize.org/nobel_prizes/medicine/laureates/2000/kandel-lecture.pdf.

180. Kandel, E.R. 1998. "A New Intellectual Framework for Psychiatry." American Journal of Psychiatry. 155(4): 457-69.

181. Kaniels, S. & Feuerstein, R. 1989. "Special Needs of Children with Learning Difficulties." Oxford Review of Education. 15 (2), pp. 165-179.

182. Kaplan-Solms K. & Solms, M. 2002. Clinical Studies in Neuro-Psychoanalysis. Karnac. NY.

183. Kazdin, A.E. 1975. "Covert Modelling, Imagery Assessment and Assertive Behaviour." Journal of Consulting and Clinical Psychology. 43, pp.716-724.

184. Kimara, D. 1973. "The Assymmetry of the Human Brain." Scientific American. 228 (3), pp. 70-80.

185. Kimara, D. September 1992. "Sex Differences in the Brain." Scientific American. pp. 119-125.

186. King, D.F. & Goodman, K.S. 1990. "Whole Language Learning, Cherishing Learners and their Language." Language, Speech and Hearing Sciences in Schools. 21, pp. 221-229.

187. Kintsch, W. 1980. "Learning from Text, Levels of Comprehension, or Why Anyone Would Read a Story Anyway?" Poetics. 9, pp. 87-98.

188. Kline, P. 1990. Everyday Genius. Great Ocean Publishers. Arlington, VA.

189. Knowles, M. 1990. The Adult Learner: A neglected species. Gulf Publishing Company. Houston.

190. Kopp, M.S. & Rethelyi, J. 2004. "Where Psychology Meets Physiology: Chronic stress and premature mortality – the Central-Eastern European health paradox." Brain Research Bulletin. 62: 351-367.
191. Kosslyn, S.M. & Koenig, O. 1995. Wet Mind: The new cognitive neuroscience. Free. NY.
192. Kubzansky, L.D., Kawachi, A. et al. 1997. "Is Worrying Bad for Your Heart? A prospective study of worry and coronary heart disease in the normative aging study." Circulation. (94):818-24.
193. Laughter. 2007. http://thehealingpoweroflaughter.blogspot.com/2007/07/how-marx-brothers-brought-norman.html.
194. Laughter. 2006. http://heyugly.org/LaughterOneSheet2.php.
195. Larsson, G. & Starrin, B. 1988. "Effect of Relaxation Training on Verbal Ability, Sequential Thinking and Spatial Ability." Journal of the Society of Accelerative Learning and Teaching. 13 (2), pp. 147-159.
196. Lahaye, T. & Noebel, D. 2000. "Mind Siege." The Battle for Truth in the New Millennium. Word Publishing. TN.
197. Lazar, C. 1994. "A Review and Appraisal of Current Information on Speech/ Language Alternative Service Delivery Models in Schools." Communiphon. 308, pp. 8-11.
198. Lazar, S.W. & Kerr, C.E. 2005. "Meditation Experience is Associated with Increased Cortical Thickness." NeuroReport. 16(17): 189-97.
199. Lea, L. 1980. Wisdom: Don't live life without it. Highland Books. Guilford, Surrey.
200. Leaf, C.M. 1985. "Mind Mapping as a Therapeutic Intervention Technique." Unpublished workshop manual.
201. Leaf, C.M. 1989. "Mind Mapping as a Therapeutic Technique." Communiphon. 296, pp. 11-15. South African Speech-Language-Hearing Association.
202. Leaf, C.M. 1990. "Teaching Children to Make the Most of Their Minds: Mind Mapping." Journal for Technical and Vocational Education in South Africa. 121, pp. 11-13.
203. Leaf, C.M. 1990. "Mind Mapping: A therapeutic technique for closed head injury." Masters Dissertation, University of Pretoria. Pretoria, SA.
204. Leaf, C.M. 1992. "Evaluation and Remediation of High School Children's Problems Using the Mind Mapping Therapeutic Approach." Remedial Teaching. Unisa, 7/8, September 1992.
205. Leaf, C.M., Uys, I.C. & Louw, B. 1992. "The Mind Mapping Approach (MMA): A culture and language-free technique." The South African Journal of Communication Disorders Vol. 40. pp. 35-43.
206. Leaf, C.M. 1993. "The Mind Mapping Approach (MMA): Open the door to your brain power: Learn how to learn." Transvaal Association of Educators Journal (TAT).
207. Leaf, C.M. 1997. "The Mind Mapping Approach: A model and framework for Geodesic Learning." Unpublished D. Phil Dissertation, University of Pretoria. Pretoria, SA.
208. Leaf, C.M. 1997. "The Development of a Model for Geodesic Learning: The Geodesic Information Processing Model." The South African Journal of Communication Disorders Vol. 44. pp. 53-70.
209. Leaf, C.M. 1997. "The Move from Institution Based Rehabilitation (IBR) to Community Based Rehabilitation (CBR): A paradigm shift." Therapy Africa. 1 (1) August 1997, p. 4.
210. Leaf, C.M. 1997. "An Altered Perception of Learning: Geodesic Learning." Therapy Africa. 1 (2), October 1997, p. 7.
211. Leaf, C.M., Uys, I. & Louw. B., 1997. "The Development of a Model for Geodesic Learning: The Geodesic Information Processing Model." The South African Journal of Communication Disorders. 44.
212. Leaf, C.M. 1998. "An Altered Perception of Learning: Geodesic Learning: Part 2." Therapy Africa. 2 (1), January/February 1998, p. 4.

213. Leaf, C.M., Uys, I.C. & Louw, B. 1998. "An Alternative Non-Traditional Approach to Learning: The Metacognitive-Mapping Approach." The South African Journal of Communication Disorders. 45, pp. 87-102.

214. Leaf. C.M. 2002. Switch on Your Brain with the Metacognitive-Mapping Approach. Truth Publishing.

215. Leaf, C.M. 2005. Switch on Your Brain: Understand your unique intelligence profile and maximize your potential. Tafelberg. Cape Town, SA.

216. Leaf, C.M. 2008. Switch on Your Brain 5 Step Learning Process. Switch on Your Brain USA. Dallas, TX.

217. Leaf, C.M. 2007. Who Switched Off My Brain? Controlling Toxic Thoughts and Emotions. Switch on Your Brain USA. Dallas, TX.

218. Leaf, C.M. 2007. "Who Switched Off My Brain? Controlling toxic thoughts and emotions." DVD series. Switch on Your Brain. Johannesburg, SA.

219. Leaf, C.M., Copeland M. & Maccaro, J. 2007. "Your Body His Temple: God's plan for achieving emotional wholeness." DVD series. Life Outreach International. Dallas, TX.

220. LeDoux, J. 2002. Synaptic Self: How our brains become who we are. NY.

221. Leedy, P.D. 1989. Practical Research: Planning and design. Macmillan. NY.

222. Lehmann, E.L. 1975. Non-Parametric: Statistical methods based on ranks. Holden-Day. CA.

223. Leuchter, A.F. & Cook, I.A. et al. 2002. "Changes in Brain Function of Depressed Subject During Treatment with Placebo." American Journal of Psychiatry. 159(1): 122-129.

224. Levy, J. 1983. "Research Synthesis on Right and Left Hemispheres: We think with both sides of the brain." Educational Leadership. 40 (4), pp. 66-71.

225. Levy, J. 1985. "Interview." Omni. 7 (4).

226. Lewis, R. 1994. "Report Back on the Workshop: Speech/language/hearing therapy in transition." Communiphon. 308, pp. 6-7.

227. Lipton, B. 2008. The Biology of Belief: Unleashing the power of consciousness, matter and miracles. Mountain of Love Productions. USA.

228. Lipton, B.H., Bensch, K.G., et al. 1991. "Microvessel Endothelial Cell Transdifferentiation: Phenotypic Characterization." Differentiation 46: 117-133.

229. Love and Neuroscience. 2009. http://www.nature.com/nature/journal/v457/n7226/full/457148a.html.

230. Lozanov, G. & Gateva, G. 1989. The Foreign Language Educator's Suggestopaedic Manual. Gordon and Breach Science Publishers. Switzerland.

231. Lozanov, G. 1978. Suggestology and Outlines of Suggestopedy. Gordon and Breach Science Publishers. NY.

232. Luria, A.R. 1980. Higher Cortical Functions in Man, 2nd Ed. Basic Books. NY.

233. Lutz, K.A. & Rigney, J.W. 1977. The Memory Book. Skin & Day. NY.

234. L.T.F.A. 1995. Unpublished Lecture Series on "Brain-Based Learning." Lead the Field Africa. SA.

235. MacLean, P. 1978. "A Mind of Three Minds: Educating the triune brain." 77th Yearbook of the National Society for the Study of Education. pp. 308-342. University of Chicago Press. Chicago.

236. Margulies, N. 1991. Mapping Inner-Space. Zephyr Press. Tulson.

237. Martin, K. 2009. www.biolchem.ucla.edu/labs/martinlab/links.htm.

238. Martin, K. 2009. http://www.foxnews.com/story/0,2933,529187,00.html.

239. Marvin, C.A. 1987. "Consultation Services: Changing roles for the SLP's." Journal of Childhood Communication Disorders. 11 (1), pp. 1-15.

240. Maslow, A.H. 1970. Motivation and Personality. Harper & Row. NY.

241. Mastropieri, M.A. & Bakken, J.P. 1990. "Applications of Metacognition." Remedial and Special Education. 11 (6) 32-35.

242. Matheny, K.B. & McCarthy, J. 2000. Prescription for Stress. Harbinger Publications. USA.

243. McEwan, B.S. 1999. "Stress and Hippocampal Plasticity." Annual Review of Neuroscience. 22:105-22.
244. McEwan, B.S. & Lasley, E.N. 2002. The End of Stress as We Know It. National Academies Press. WA.
245. McEwan, B.S. & Seeman, T. 1999. "Protective & Damaging Effects of Mediators of Stress: Elaborating and testing the concepts of allostasis and allostatic load." Annals of the New York Academy of Sciences. 896:30-47.
246. McGaugh, J.L. & Intrioni-Collision, I.B. 1990. "Involvement of the Amygdaloidal Complex in Neuromodulatory Influences on Memory Storage." Neuroscience and Behavioral Reviews. 14 (4), pp. 425-431.
247. Merzenich, M. 2009. http://merzenich.positscience.com/.
248. Merzenich, M.M. 2001. "Cortical Plasticity Contributing to Childhood Development." in McClelland, J.L. & Siegler R.S. (Eds.) Mecheanisms of Cognitive Development: Behavioral and Neural Perspectives. Lawrence Eribaum Associates. Mahwah, NJ.
249. Meyer, J. 1995. The Battlefield of the Mind. Faith Words. USA.
250. Meyer, J. 2000. Life without Strife: How God can heal and restore troubled relationships. Charisma House. FL.
251. Miller, G.A. 1956. "The Magical Number Seven, Plus or Minus Two: Some limits on our capacity for processing information." Psychological Review, 63, pp. 81-97.
252. Miller, T. & Sabatino, D. 1978. "An Evaluation of the Educator Consultant Model as an Approach to Main Streaming." Exceptional Children, 45.
253. "Mind/Body Connection: How emotions affect your health." 2009. http://family doctor.org/online/famdocen/home/healthy/mental/782.html.
254. Mogilner, A., Grossman, J.A. et al. 1993. Somatosensory Cortical Plasticity in Adult Humans Revealed by Magneto Encephalography. Proceedings of the National Academy of Sciences, USA 90(8): 3593-97.
255. Montessori, M. 1989. The Absorbent Mind. Clio Press. Amsterdam.
256. Mountcastle, V. 1978. "An Organizing Principle for Cerebral Function: The unit module and the distributed system." in McAllister. 2000. "Cellular and Molecular Mechanisms of Dendritic Growth." Cerebral Cortex, 10(10): 963-73. Oxford University Press.
257. Nader, K., Schafe, G.E. et al. 2000. "Fear Memories Require Protein Synthesis in the Amygdala for Reconsolidation after Retrieval." Nature. 406(6797): 722-26.
258. National Institute of Mental Health. 2009. www.nimh.nih.gov/health/topics/statistics/index.shtml.
259. Nelson, A. 1988. "Imagery's Physiological Base: The limbic system. A review paper." Journal of the Society for Accelerative Learning and Teaching. 13 (4), pp 363-371.
260. Nelson, R. (Ed.) 1992. Metacognition Core Readings. Allyn & Bacon. Needham Heights, MA.
261. Neuroscience Review. http://cumc.columbia.edu/dept/cme/neuroscience/neuro/speakers.html.
262. Newberg, A., D'Aquili, E. et al. 2001. "Why God Won't Go Away: Brain science and the biology of belief." Ballantine. NY.
263. Novak, J.D. & Gowin, B. 1984. Learning How to Learn. Cambridge University Press. Cambridge.
264. Nummela, R.M. & Rosengren, T.M. 1985. "Orchestration of Internal Processing." Journal for the Society of Accelerated Learning and Teaching. 10 (2), pp. 89-97.
265. Odendaal, M.S. 1985. "Needs Analysis of Higher Primary Educators in KwaZulu." Per Linguam, Special Issue No.1. pp. 5-99.
266. Okebukola, P.A. 1992. "Attitudes of Educators Towards Concept Mapping and Vee-diagramming as Metalearning Tools in Science and Mathematics." Educational Research, 34 (3), pp. 201-212.
267. O'keefe, J. & Nadel, L. 1978. The Hippocampus as a Cognitive Map. Oxford University Press. NY.

268. Olivier, C. 1999. Let's Educate, Train and Learn Outcomes-Based. Benedic. Pretoria, SA.
269. Olsen, K.E. 1997. Outcomes Based Education: An experiment in social engineering. Christians for Truth. SA.
270. Ornstein, R.E. 1975. The Psychology of Consciousness. Penguin Books. NY.
271. Ornstein, R. 1997. The Right Mind. Harcourt, Brace and Company. Orlando, FL.
272. Palincsar, A.S. & Brown, A.L. 1984. "Reciprocal Teaching of Comprehension Fostering and Monitoring Activities." Cognition and Instruction. 1, pp. 117-175.
273. Palmer, L.L., Alexander, M. & Ellis, N. 1989. "Elementary School Achievement Results Following In-Service Training of an Entire School Staff in Accelerative Learning and Teaching: An interim report." Journal of the Society for Accelerative Learning and Teaching. 14 (1), pp. 55-79.
274. Paris, S.G. & Winograd, P. 1990. "Promoting Metacognition and Motivation of Exceptional Children." Remedial and Special Education. 11 (6), pp. 7-15.
275. Pascuale-Leone, A. & Hamilton, R. 2001. "The Metamodal Organization of the Brain." in Casanova, C. & Ptito. (Eds.) Progress in Brain Research Volume 134. Elsevier Science. San Diego, CA.
276. Paul-Brown, D. 1992. "Professional Practices Perspective on Alternative Service Delivery Models." ASHA Bulletin. 12.
277. Perlemutter, D. & Coleman, C. 2004. The Better Brain Book. Penguin Group. USA.
278. Pert, C. B. 1997. Molecules of Emotion: Why you feel the way you feel. Simon and Schuster. UK.
279. Pert, C. et al. 1973. "Opiate Agonists and Antagonists Discriminated by Receptor Binding in the Brain." Science. (182): 1359-61.
280. Peters, T. 2003. Playing God? Genetic Determinism and Human Freedom, 2nd Ed. Routledge. NY.
281. "The Pleasure Centers Affected by Drugs." http://thebrain.mcgill.ca/flash/i/i_03/i_03_cr/i_03_cr_par/i_03_cr_par.html.
282. Plotsky, P.M. & Meaney, M.J. 1993. "Early Postnatal Experience Alters Hypothalamic Corticotrophin-releasing Factor (CRF) mRNA, Median Eminence CRF Content and Stress-induced Release in Adult Rats." Molecular Brain Research. 18:195-200.
283. Policy Document, 2002. "Revised National Curriculum Statement Grades R-9." Department of Education. Pretoria, SA.
284. Praag, A.F., Schinder, B.R. et al. 2002. "Functional Neurogenesis in the Adult Hippocampus." Nature. 415(6875): 1030-34.
285. Pribram, K.H. 1971. Languages of the Brain. Brooks/Cole. Monterey, CA.
286. Pulvermuller, F. 2002. The Neuroscience of Language. Cambridge University Press.
287. Rajechi, D.W. 1982. Attitudes: Themes and Advances. Sinauer Associates. Sunderland, MA.
288. Ramachandran, V.S. & Blakeslee, S. 1998. Phantoms in the Brain. William Morrow. NY.
289. Redding, R.E. 1990. "Metacognitive Instruction: Trainers teaching thinking skills." Performance Improvement Quarterly. 3 (1), pp. 27-41.
290. Relax. 2005. http://www.scientificamerican.com/article.cfm?id=want-clear-thinking-relax&page=2.
291. Relaxation. 2005. http://www.scientificamerican.com/article.cfm?id=want-clear-thinking-relax.
292. Religion and Science. 2009. http://www.time.com/time/health/article/\0,8599,1879016,00.html.
293. Religion and Science. 2008. http://www.liebertonline.com/doi/abs/10.1089/acm.2007.0675.
294. Restak, K. 1979. The Brain: The last frontier. Doubleday. NY.
295. Restak, R. 2000. "Mysteries of the Mind." National Geographic Society.
296. Restak, R. 2009. Think Smart: A neuroscientists prescription for improving your brain performance. Riverhead Books. NY.
297. Rizzolotti, G. 2008. http://www.scholarpedia.org/article/Mirror_neurons.
298. Rogers, C.R. 1969. Freedom to Learn. Merrill. Columbus, OH.

299. Rosenfield, I. 1988. The Invention of Memory. Basic Books. NY.

300. Rosenzweig, M.R. & Bennet, E.L. 1976. Neuronal Mechanisms of Learning and Memory. MIT Press. Cambridge, MA.

301. Rosenzweig, E.S., Barnes, C.A., & McNaughton, B.L. 2002. "Making Room for New Memories." Nature Neuroscience. 5(1): 6-8.

302. Rozin, P. 1975. "The Evolution of Intelligence and Access to the Cognitive Unconscious." Progress in Psychobiology and Physiological Psychology. 6, pp. 245-280.

303. Russell, P. 1986. The Brain Book. Routledge & Kegan Paul. London.

304. Rutherford, R. & Neethling, K. 2001. Am I Clever or Am I Stupid? Carpe Diem Books. Van-derbijlpark.

305. Sagan, C. 1977. The Dragons of Eden. Random House. NY.

306. Saloman, G. 1979. Interaction of Media, Cognition and Learning. Jossey-Bass. San Francisco, CA.

307. Samples, R.E. 1975. "Learning with the Whole Brain." Human Behavior. 4, pp. 16-23.

308. Sapolsky, R.M. 1996. "Why Stress is Bad for Your Brain." Science. 273(5276): 749-50.

309. Sarno, J. 1999. The Mind-Body Prescription. Werner Books. NY.

310. Schallert, D.L. 1982. "The Significance of Knowledge: A synthesis of research related to schema theory." in Otto, W. & White, S. (Eds.) Reading Expository Material. pp. 13-48. Academic. NY.

311. Schneider, W. & Shiffrin, R.M. 1977. "Controlled and Automatic Information Processing: I: Detection, search and attention." Psychological Review. 88, pp. 1-66.

312. Schon, D.A. 1971. Beyond the Stable State. Jossey-Bass. San Francisco, CA.

313. Schory, M.E. 1990. "Whole Language and the Speech Language Pathologists in Language, Speech and Hearing Services in Schools." 21, pp. 206-211.

314. Schuster, D.H. 1985. "A Critical Review of American Foreign Language Studies Using Suggestopaedia." Paper delivered at the Aimav Linguistic Conference at the University of Nijmegen, The Netherlands.

315. Schwartz, J.M. & Begley, S. 2002. The Mind and the Brain: Neuroplasticity and the power of mental force. Regan Books/Harper Collins. NY.

316. Scruggs, E. & Brigham, J. 1987. "The Challenges of Metacognitive Instruction." RASE. 11 (6), pp. 16-18.

317. Seaward, B. L. 1996. Health and Wellness Journal Workbook.

318. Segerstrom, S.C. & Miller, G.E. 2004. "Psychological Stress and the Human Immune System: A meta-analytic study of 30 years of inquiry." Psychological Bulletin Vol 130. N04. 601-630.

319. Shapiro, R.B., Champagne, V.G. & De Costa, D. 1988. "The Speech-language Pathologist: Consultant to the classroom educator." Reading Improvement. 25 (1), pp. 2-9.

320. Sheth, B.R. 2006. "Practice Makes Imperfect: Restorative effects of sleep on motor learning." Society for Neuroscience. Program 14-14.

321. Simon, C.S. 1987. "Out of the Broom Closet and into the Classroom: The Emerging SLP." Journal of Childhood Communication Disorders. 11 (1-2), pp. 81-90.

322. Singer, T. 2004. "How Your Brain Handles Love and Pain." http://www.msnbc.msn.com/id/4313263.

323. Sizer, T.R. 1984. Horacel's Compromise: The dilemma of the American high school. Houghton Mifflin. Boston.

324. Slabbert, J. 1989. "Metalearning as the Most Essential Aim in Education for All." Paper presented at University of Pretoria, Faculty of Education. Pretoria, SA.

325. Sleep. 2003. http://www.applesforhealth.com/lacksleep1.html.

326. Slife, B.D., Weiss, J. & Bell, T. 1985. "Separability of Metacognition and Cognition: Problem solving in learning disabled and regular students." Journal of Educational Psychology. 77 (4), pp. 437-445.

327. Smith, A. 1999. Accelerated Learning in Practice. Network Educational Press. Stafford, UK.

328. Sperry, R. 1968. "Hemisphere Disconnection and Unity in Conscious Awareness." American Psychologist. 23 (1968).
329. Solms, M. 1999. http://www.abc.net.au/rn/talks/8.30/helthrpt/stories/s44369.htm.
330. Solms, M. 2000. "Forebrain Mechanisms of Dreaming are Activated from a Variety of Sources." Behavioral and Brain Sciences. 23 (6): 1035-1040; 1083-1121.
331. Spitz, R. 1983. http://www.pep-web.org/document.php?id=PPSY.002.0181A.
332. Springer, S.P. & Deutsch, G. 1998. Left Brain, Right Brain. W.H. Freeman & Company. NY.
333. Stephan, K.M., Fink, G.R. et al. 1995. "Functional Anatomy of Mental Representation of Upper Extremity Movements in Healthy Subjects." Journal of Neurophysiology. 73(1): 373-86.
334. Sternberg, R. 1979. "The Nature of Mental Abilities." American Psychologist. 34, pp. 214-230.
335. Stickgold, R., Hobson, R. et al. 2001. "Sleep, Learning, and Dreams: Offline memory reprocessing." Science. 294 (554): 1052-57.
336. Stickgold, R. & Wehrwein, P. 2009. "Sleep Now, Remember Later." Newsweek. http://www.newsweek.com/id/194650.
337. Stress in Children. www.cookchildrens.org.
338. Sylwester, R. 1985. "Research on Memory: Major discoveries, major educational challenges." Educational Leadership. pp. 69-75.
339. Tattershall, S. 1987. "Mission Impossible: Learning how a classroom works before it's too late!" Journal of Childhood Communication Disorders. 11 (1), pp. 181-184.
340. Taubes, G. 2008. Good Calories, Bad Calories: Fats, carbs and the controversial science of diet and health. Anchor Books. NY.
341. Taub, E., Uswatte, G. et al. 2005. "Use of CI Therapy for Plegic Hands after Chronic Stroke." Presentation at the Society for neuroscience. Washington D.C.
342. Thembela, A. 1990. "Education for Blacks in South Africa: Issues, problems and perspectives." Journal of the Society for Accelerative Learning and Teaching. 15 (12), pp. 45-57.
343. Thurman, S.K. & Widerstrom, A.H. 1990. Infants and Young Children with Special Needs: A developmental and ecological approach, (2nd Ed.). Paul H. Brookes. Baltimore, MD.
344. Tunajek, S. 2006. "The Attitude Factor." http://www.aana.com/uploadedFiles/Resources/Wellness/nb_milestone_0406.pdf.
345. "Understanding the Different Types of Depression." 2002. www.Depression-Anxiety.com.
346. Uys, I.C. 1989. "Single Case Experimental Designs: An essential service in communicatively disabled care." The South African Journal of Communication Disorders. 36, pp. 53-59.
347. Van derVyfer, D.W. 1985. "SALT in South Africa: Needs and parameters." Journal of the Society for Accelerative Learning and Teaching. 10(3), pp. 187-200.
348. Van derVyver, D.W. & de Capdeville, B. 1990. "Towards the Mountain: Characteristics and implications of the South African UPPTRAIL pilot project." Journal of the Society for Accelerative Learning and Teaching. 15 (1 & 2), pp. 59-74.
349. Vaughan, S.C. 1997. The Talking Cure: The science behind psychotherapy. Grosset/Putnam. NY.
350. Vaynman S., & Gomez-Pinilla. 2005. "License to Run: Exercise impacts functional plasticity in the intact and injured central nervous system by using neurotrophins." Neurorehabilitation and Neural Repair. 19(4): 283-95.
351. Von Bertalanaffy, L. 1968. General Systems Theory. Braziller. NY.
352. Vythilingam, M. & Heim, C. "Childhood Trauma Associated with Smaller Hippocampal Volume in Women with Major Depression." American Journal of Psychiatry. 159(12): 2072-80.
353. Walker, M.P. & Stickgold, R. 2006. "Sleep, Memory and Plasticity." Annual Review of Psychology.

354.Wark, D.M. 1986. "Using Imagery to Teach Study Skills." Journal of the Society for Accelerative Learning and Teaching. 11 (3), pp. 203-220.
355.Waterland, R.A. & Jirtle, R.L. 2003. "Transposable Elements: Targets for early nutritional effects on epigenetic gene regulation." Molecular and Cellular Biology. 23(15): 5293-5300.
356.Wenger, W. 1985. "An Example of Limbic Learning." Journal of the Society for Accelerative Learning and Teaching. 10 (1), pp. 51-68.
357.Wertsch, J.V. 1985. Culture, Communication and Cognitions. NY.
358.Whitelson, S. 1985. "The Brain Connection: The corpus callosum is larger in left-handers." Science. 229, pp. 665-8.
359.Widener, C. 2004. The Angel Inside. E Books. www.theangelinside.com.
360.Wilson, R.S., Mendes, C.F. et al. 2002. "Participation in Cognitively Stimulating Activities and Risk of Incident in Alzheimer's Disease." JAMA. 287(6): 742-48.
361.Wright, N.H. 2005. Finding Freedom from Your Fears. Fleming H. Revell. Grand Rapids.
362.Wurtman, J. 1986. Managing Your Mind-Mood through Food. Harper/Collins. NY.
363.Zaidel, E. 1985. "Roger Sperry: An Appreciation." in Benson, D.F. & Zaidel, E. (Eds.). The Dual Brain. The Guilford Press. NY.
364.Zakaluk, B.L. & Klassen, M. 1992. "Enhancing the Performance of a High School Student Labelled Learning Disabled." Journal of Reading. 36 (1).
365.Zdenek, M. 1983. The Right Brain Experience. McGraw-Hill. Great Britain.
366.Zimmerman, B.J. & Schunk, D.H. 1989. Self-Regulated Learning and Academic Achievement: Theory, research and practice. Springer-Verby. NY.

p 20 Neurons
p 30 Dendrites
p 33 Neuron tree